21 DAYS OF PRAYER & FASTING

HOW TO SEEK GOD WITH PURPOSE, POWER, AND PERSISTENCE

THOMAS M. TWIGG JR.

This book is intended for informational and educational purposes only. The views and opinions expressed are those of the author and do not necessarily reflect those of any organization or individual referenced. Nothing in this book should be construed as professional, legal, financial, medical, or spiritual advice. Readers are encouraged to seek qualified counsel before making decisions based on the content of this book.

Any references to real people, organizations, or events are used for illustrative purposes only. Unless otherwise stated, names, characters, places, and incidents are either the product of the author's imagination or used in a fictitious manner. Any resemblance to actual persons, living or dead, or actual events is coincidental.

Copyright © 2026 | Thomas Twigg

All rights reserved. No part of this publication may be reproduced, distributed, or transmitted in any form or by any means, including photocopying, recording, or other electronic or mechanical methods, without the prior written permission of the publisher, except in the case of brief quotations embodied in critical reviews and certain other noncommercial uses permitted by copyright law. For permission requests, write to the publisher, addressed "Attention: Permissions Coordinator," at the address below.

Paperback: 978-1-951475-49-9
Ebook: 9781951475505

First paperback edition January 2026

Arrow Press Publishing
Charleston, SC

www.arrowpresspublishing.com

CONTENTS

INTRODUCTION 5

DAY 1
Understanding Fasting 7

DAY 2
The Positioning of the Heart. 27

DAY 3
The Opening of Our Eyes. 33

DAY 4
The Denying of Our Flesh 37

DAY 5
The Faith of a Mustard Seed: Quantity or Quality? 43

DAY 6
Hungry, and Hungering for the Word of God 47

DAY 7
Sincerely Seeking God 53

DAY 8
Worshipping and Fasting. 57

DAY 9
Spitting Seeds, Picking Bones, and Having Onion Breath 65

DAY 10
Don't Falter, Faint, or Fail! 71

DAY 11
Pride, Pretense, or Passion 75

DAY 12
Fasting For a Spiritual Breakthrough 79

DAY 13
Fasting and Your Body 85

DAY 14
Fasting and Prayer 91

DAY 15
The Warfare of Fasting and Prayer 97

DAY 16
Fasting for Decision Making 103

DAY 17
The Necessity of Waiting on God 107

DAY 18
Signs, Wonders, Miracles, and Gifts of the Holy Spirit 111

DAY 19
Fasting and the Pouring Out of the Soul 115

DAY 20
Fasting and Praying Before God 119

DAY 21
Fasting and Revival 123

Closing Thought 137

Endnotes 139

INTRODUCTION

Throughout parts of the world, many churches embrace the biblical principle of fasting in conjunction with prayer as part of their agenda for the first twenty-one days of the New Year. Fasting is a powerful means of aligning our hearts to seek God and to move into a deeper intimacy with the Lord. Jesus declared that when the bridegroom was absent, his children would fast, and he also placed his approval upon fasting, stating, "When you fast," not "if you fast." The Lord anticipated that the church would fast.

Fasting and prayer is also a powerful means of overcoming the "Wicked One" and pulling down his demonic strongholds. In addition, some of God's dear children facing severe trials and adverse circumstances, such as physical, financial, and emotional crises, have resorted to prayer and fasting, and have discovered the power of prayer and fasting in the process.

Are you content to enter a new year without seeing things change in your life? If not, then I challenge you to join with a body of believers for twenty-one days of fasting and prayer. I challenge you to believe that God will do a powerful work in your life, equip you to be an overcomer, and use you to advance His Kingdom.

DAY 1: UNDERSTANDING FASTING

Notice: The subject matter for the first day is quite lengthy in comparison to the remaining twenty days, and I ask for your patience. It is lengthy due to the importance of laying down a biblical, spiritual, theological, and practical foundation for fasting.

"Is this not the fast that I have chosen: To loose the bonds of wickedness, To undo the heavy burdens, to let the oppressed go free, And that you break every yoke? Is it not to share your bread with the hungry, And that you bring to your house the poor who are cast out; When you see the naked, that you cover him, And not hide yourself from your own flesh? Then your light shall break forth like the morning, Your healing shall spring forth speedily, And your righteousness shall go before you, The glory of the LORD shall be your rear guard."

ISAIAH 58: 6-8, NKJV

"Corporate fasts are dynamic because they bring in an element of accountability, encouragement, and mobilization for greater breakthrough."[1]
-JENNIFER A. MISKOV, PH.D.

21 DAYS OF FASTING AND PRAYER

This is the first day of your fast. This may be the first time you have fasted or the first time you have entered a corporate 21-day fast. The preceding text may act as an on-ramp to fasting while providing you with eleven practical benefits of fasting. God was speaking to the nation of Israel. He defined true fasting and the benefits associated with practicing this spiritual discipline. In the 21st century, these scriptures may also apply to Christ's church. Note these benefits as you fast and pray. They are: (1) To loosen the bonds of wickedness, (2) To undo heavy burdens, (3) To let the oppressed go free, (4) To break every yoke, (5) To give bread to the hungry, (6) To clothe the naked, (7) To provide the poor with housing, (8) To allow God's light to break forth like the morning, (9) To cause healing and health to break forth speedily, (10) To cause their righteous testimony to go before them, and (11) To make the glory of the Lord a rear guard (protection).

Let's dive deeper into the subject of fasting. Some people have stated that they are fasting from certain activities, such as watching television or using social media. It would be better to refer to this as "abstaining from" instead of "fasting from." Such abstaining would demand discipline. Such abstaining would enable one to use time once invested in legitimate desires and pleasurable things and focus on hungering and thirsting after God.

Abstaining from certain activities can be profitable, as one diverts time and energy to select spiritual activities, such as reading the Word of God and prayer. Jeremiah, the prophet, proclaimed a wonderful promise, "And ye shall seek me, and find me, when you seek me with all your heart" (Jeremiah 29:13, KJV).

DAY 1

Some people have viewed fasting as a crash diet for weight loss, while others have viewed it as a way to prevent bodily diseases. Still others have used fasting as a political means to draw attention to issues they may or may not agree with. And then, some people erroneously declare that Jesus commanded Christians to fast. Jesus expected Christians to fast, but He did not strictly command fasting.

Fasting is "voluntary abstinence from *food* (emphasis mine)."[2] Or we could define fasting as a voluntary abstinence from food for a designated time and purpose. In the Old Testament, the main Hebrew word used is *tsom,* which means "to abstain from food." The Hebrew word has the connotation, "to cover your mouth.[3]" In the New Testament, the Greek word translated "fast" is *nested,* which means "to abstain from eating." In both testaments, fasting is simply going without food to seek God for some special reason.[4]

The challenge of corporate fasting for 21 days within Christian circles occurs when Christians discipline themselves by abstaining from food for *spiritual* purposes. Such churches engage in 21 days of corporate fasting by deliberately selecting the first three weeks of January. They prioritize the first three weeks of the month to God and commit the ensuing events of the year to Him. They believe Him to meet every need or situation that occurs throughout the year. It is like the setting of a sail that anticipates the blessing of the winds that enable a ship to travel on its charted course. It is a preparatory and disciplined act of expectation.

In the Old Testament, the Jews presented an offering of "first fruits" to God. In this practice, individuals willingly gave the first and best portions of their harvest to Jehovah God. The offering symbolized their genuine gratitude to God for all He had provided and acknowledged everything that came from Him. It demonstrated their commitment to prioritizing God by giving the best of their provisions and set the tone for the rest of the harvest yet to come.

Jentezen Franklin stated, "When you enter a fast at the beginning of the year with the body of Christ, you link up with thousands of people all over the world who also begin the New Year with a fast. One person fasting is powerful, but when a group of people fast, it is multiplied strength! It is multiplied power."[5] Think how exponentially powerful this can be! One ox can pull 5,000 pounds, but two oxen yoked together can pull 15,000 pounds.

Have you ever heard of draft horses? They are beautiful and powerful horses. There are several different breeds. The Clydesdale is one of the most familiar breeds. These horses weigh approximately a ton. These magnificently muscular horses can haul up to 8,000 pounds. However, two draft horses working together can exponentially pull 24,000 pounds. That is three times as much weight as one horse can tow. Even better, when two draft horses train and work together, they can pull up to 32,000 pounds, which is four times the weight each horse could move individually.[6]

I can only imagine the exponential spiritual power that will be unleashed for the promotion of the kingdom of God as you and your church join with other churches around the globe for 21 days of fasting and prayer. Jenifer A. Miskov wrote, "Many times corporate fasts, coupled with prayer and worship, bring a powerful focus,

DAY 1

synergy, and acceleration in the things of God."[7] Paul joyfully and triumphantly declared, "Now to Him who is able to do exceedingly abundantly above all we ask or think, according to the power that works in us" (Ephesians 3:10, NKJV).

The Old Testament mentions two types (or atmospheres) of fasting: private fasting and public (corporate) fasting. The Jewish requirement to observe the Day of Atonement (Yom Kippur), which occurs on the tenth day of the seventh month (Leviticus 23:27), includes observing the corporate fast. It was a day set aside for the Israelites to "afflict" or humble their souls.

Although nowhere in the books of Moses is there an explanation of "afflicting the soul" required on the Day of Atonement (Lev. 23:27,29,32 KJV), the Jews have continuously interpreted it to mean fasting (Ps. 35:13; Is. 58:3, 5, 10).[8] It was considered a "holy convocation," i.e., a gathering of like-minded believers. In Christian circles, a twenty-one-day period of prayer and fasting is voluntary and not mandated. Such holy convocations can be a powerful experience as like-minded people gather in prayer and fasting and believe God to do great things in their church, community, and city.

At other times, a corporate fast was begun during difficult times and was viewed as a national emergency. For example, when King Jehoshaphat learned of a coming invasion of Judah, he summoned a corporate fast. And when the king of Nineveh heard of the impending judgment upon his nation, he also called for corporate fasting. These corporate fasts, in which people gathered with one mind, resulted in a powerful move of God.

Jeremiah had written of judgment upon Judah, Israel, and the surrounding nations. He sought to warn the people by sending Baruch to read the prophetic words in the temple on the day of fasting. Jeremiah's heart yearned for the people to heed the warning and turn from their evil ways, so that God would forgive their sins. Jehoiakim, king of Judah, proclaimed a national fast for the people from the cities of Judah to Jerusalem (Jeremiah 36).

In his book, *Celebration of Discipline,* Richard Foster wrote that in 1756, the King of Britain faced an imminent invasion by the French. The king called for a day of solemn prayer and fasting, and according to John Wesley, every church in the city was more than full. The humility of the British resulted in a day of rejoicing because the threatened invasion was averted.[9]

In 2001, two hijacked planes crashed into the Twin Towers of the World Trade Center in New York. I watched on television as the towers collapsed, killing thousands of people. It was a national disaster. I was pastoring a church in Edgewood, Maryland. I recall many churches in which attendance increased beyond the norm as people assembled to pray.

In times of a national economic crisis, people have often resorted to prayer and fasting. The combination of prayer and fasting produces the most powerful weapon to be employed individually or collectively by God's people during spiritual warfare. Israel was living during a time of great economic pressure. Crops were failing, livestock suffered from the lack of water and food, and the priesthood lacked the provisions to perform a meat offering or drink offering

DAY 1

unto the Lord. So, Joel called for the nation to sanctify a fast. "Blow the trumpet in Zion, consecrate a fast; call a solemn assembly; gather the people" (Joel 2:16, ESV). It was a solemn assembly in which the Lord said, "Return to me with all your heart with fasting, with weeping, and with mourning," and rend your hearts and not your garments" (Joel 2:12-13, ESV).

But we do not have to wait for a national crisis to pray and fast. Churches can set aside the first 21 days of each new year to gather to pray and fast. It can be a time when people draw closer to God. It can be a time when people experience the blessings of God in their lives, and the kingdom of God expands in their community.

Many Christians select the first hour or hours of the day for prayer and reading the Word of God. In doing so, they set the course of their day by committing the events that occur in the day to the Lord. As we have stated, Jesus did not command us to fast, but he expected us to fast. However, God commanded us to pray. The Scriptures are replete with commands to pray. Here are just three: "Call unto me and I will answer you and show thee great and mighty things which thou knowest not" (Jeremiah 33:3-4, KJV). "Watch and pray lest ye enter into temptation" (Mark 14:38, KJV). Pray without ceasing" (I Thessalonians 5:17, KJV). Charles Spurgeon, in his book entitled *Prayer and Spiritual Warfare,* wrote:

> God's own people need a command to pray, or else they would not receive it. How is this? Because, dear friends, we are subject to fits of worldliness, if indeed that is not our usual state. We do not forget to eat. We do not forget to be diligent in business. We

do not forget to get our rest. But we forget to wrestle with God in prayer and to spend, as we ought to spend, long periods in consecrated fellowship with our Father and our God.[10]

Dick Eastman wrote, "Fasting is the practice of deliberately abstaining from usual nourishment for the purpose of adding power to our prayer as well as stimulating our spiritual growth".[11] Fasting could be for a spiritual breakthrough. It could be for breaking strongholds. It could be for a spiritual awakening in the church and community. It could be for a spiritual awakening in the nations of the world. It could be for seeking God for wisdom while facing a severe trial.

Perhaps one of the greatest purposes of fasting and prayer is to seek a deeper understanding of God and to know God more intimately. Jesus said, "Blessed are they that hunger and thirst after righteousness, for they shall be filled" (Matthew 5:6, KJV). When a Christian abstains from food and earnestly fasts and prays for 21 days, it is a sincere demonstration of wanting to have a personal relationship with God, to know Him, and not simply to know about Him.

These spiritual purposes are more than pious wishes. Christians recognize they are not wrestling "against flesh and blood, but against principalities, against powers, against rulers of darkness of this world, against spiritual wickedness in high places" (Ephesians 6:12, KJV).

A religious group of people called Pharisees presented the subject of fasting to Jesus. "And they said to him, the disciples of John fast often and offer prayers, and so do the disciples of the Pharisees, but yours eat and drink" (Luke 5:33, ESV). Jesus responded, "Can you make wedding guests fast while the bridegroom is with them? The

DAY 1

days will come when the bridegroom is taken away from them, and then they will fast in those days (Luke 5:34-35, ESV).

Christ also revealed his expectation of fasting when he delivered his sermon on the Mount. "And when you fast, do not look gloomy like the hypocrites, for they disfigure their faces that their fasting may be seen by others. Truly, I say to you, they have received their reward. But when you fast, anoint your head and wash your face, that your fasting may not be seen by others but by your Father who is in secret. And your Father who sees in secret will reward you" (Matthew 6:16-17, ESV).

Some people with medical conditions, such as diabetes, heart conditions, low blood sugar, or any other medical problems, should consult with their doctor before fasting. Similarly, expectant mothers should consult with their doctors before fasting.

This first day may be physically difficult, depending on the type of fast you are following. The Bible mentions four kinds of fasts: the normal, absolute, partial, and supernatural.

The Normal Fast (the food fast)

Having established that the biblical terminology for *fasting* is a reference to abstaining from food (solid and liquid foods). The normal fast is a fast in which a person abstains from all food. For most people, this would mean not eating three meals during the day or eating snacks between meals.

Jesus, according to most theologians and Bible scholars, would have done a normal fast that lasted 40 days. There is no indication that he abstained from drinking water. We may also note that when Satan tempted Jesus, he did not bring up the subject of drinking water.

Technically speaking (though we do not know for how long), the first known normal fast mentioned in the Bible is that of Abraham's servant. "Then food was set before him to eat. But he said, 'I will not eat until I have said what I have to say,'" (Genesis 24:33, NIV). While the timeline is unclear, Rebekah took time to water his camels. After the camels were watered, a conversation ensued in which he inquired about her identity and whether there was room in her father's house for him to spend the night. We do not know how far the well was from Rebekah's home and how long it took to get there. Time passed as Abraham's servant rehearsed his mission and Rebekah's arrival at the well. After receiving permission to take Rebekah to Isaac, he took time to distribute gifts to her family. Following these events, we read, "And he and the men who were with him ate and drank, and they spent the night there" (Genesis 24:54, ESV).

We see a normal three-day fast under the leadership of Ezra. Ezra led a second group of people who traveled from Babylon to Jerusalem during the reign of Artaxerxes. Among the 1,850+ people who gathered at the river Ahava, twelve priests were chosen and entrusted with a free-will offering of silver, gold, and sacred articles to be taken to the house of God in Jerusalem.

Ezra felt a responsibility for the people, their possessions, and the wealth entrusted to him to be given to the temple and its services. The route would be dangerous. Thieves and bandits roamed the area. This responsibility must have weighed heavily on his heart. Listen to his

DAY 1

heart cry, "There, by the river Ahava Canal, I proclaimed a fast, so that we might humble ourselves before our God and ask him of a safe journey for us and our children, with all our possessions" (Ezra, 8:21).

This caravan came to a halt, and they stopped what they were doing and fasted. What a sight to see all the tents erected along a riverbank and some 1850 + people fasting and praying for three days (Ezra 8:15). Sometimes we must stop what we are doing, realize our situation in life, and employ the mercies of God. The greater the responsibility, the greater the measures we must take. What great responsibilities are you overseeing? Is it a company, a church, a corporation, a new business, a new job, or a new position? Perhaps you feel insecure or anxious? Why not set aside some time for fasting and prayer?

Not only did Ezra feel the responsibility of the people, but he had also made a very bold statement. He had stated to King Artaxerxes, "The gracious hand of our God is on everyone who looks to him, but his great anger is against all who forsake him." In doing so, he felt ashamed to ask the king for soldiers and horsemen to protect the caravan from enemies on the road. He had essentially declined a military escort to Jerusalem.

Have you ever made a bold statement by faith or committed to something bigger than your ability? Ezra depended on the gracious and omnipotent hand of God. Perhaps his faith was wavering just a little at this point. Perhaps he was questioning the bold statement of faith he had made. What could he do? He stood on his statement, "The gracious hand of our God is on everyone who LOOKS TO

HIM" (Ezra 8:22). He sought to buttress his faith with fasting and prayer. He encouraged himself and the people to humble themselves before God with prayer and fasting for three days.

Fasting is more than seeking to get God's attention. Fasting is when we seek Him and give Him our attention by humbling our hearts before Him in prayer. It is never a time when we aim to earn anything. It is a time to lean on Him. Throughout the Scriptures, we find God responds to a broken and contrite heart. When we humble our souls in fasting, God takes notice, but fasting is never to be interpreted as earning God's attention.

Ezra could joyfully say, "So we fasted and petitioned our God about this, and He answered our prayer" (Ezra 8:23). What is the urgent "THIS" in your life? God is interested in turning your "THIS" into a "THAT". Like Ezra, you can say, "I humbled my soul, prayed, and petitioned God, and I can assure you, "THAT" He answered my prayer!

Jehoshaphat, king of Judah, was informed of a great multitude of enemy soldiers coming against him for battle. When he heard the disturbing news, he was afraid. To his credit, Jehoshaphat had a godly father, Asa, who in his early years of reigning over Judah "did that which was good and right in the eyes of the Lord" (II Chronicles 14:27). And when an army from Ethiopia of a million men and 300 chariots came against him, he cried out to God for help and God helped him defeat the vast army.

Jehoshaphat knew of God's mighty intervention; his father had experienced it. He knew about his Daddy's prayer! Being afraid, Je-

DAY 1

hoshaphat knew what he could do. He "set his face to seek the Lord and proclaimed a fast throughout all Judah. All the cities of Judah came to seek the Lord" (II Chronicles 20:3). We are not told how long the fast was and what kind of a fast it was. It could very well have been a normal fast.

God showed up! The Spirit of the Lord came upon Jahaziel. He told them not to be afraid of the great army advancing because the battle was not theirs but the Lord's. He prophesied that they would not have to fight the battle. God sent an ambush against the invading army, and they fought each other. The victory was so great that it took Judah three days to gather the spoil (II Chronicles 20:15-17, ESV).

What fears are you facing? Whatever trial you are facing, try fasting and prayer. God takes note when you humble your heart, pray, and fast before Him. He answers prayer not because of who we are but because of who He is. He is an infinitely good and merciful God who loves his children.

King Ahab conducted another normal fast. He was a wicked king. The Bible, in describing his wickedness, states, "There was none who sold himself to do what was evil in the sight of the Lord like Ahab, whom Jezebel his wife incited" (I Kings 21:12, ESV). God sent Elijah to inform Ahab of the impending judgment and disaster that was coming upon him. Elijah declared Ahab had sold himself to do evil in the sight of the Lord and had caused Israel to sin.

Although Ahab was wicked; when he heard the prophetic word of Elijah concerning his future judgment, "He tore his clothes, put sackcloth on his flesh, fasted, and lay in sackcloth and went about dejectedly" (I Kings 21: 27). We are not told the length of his fasting or that he abstained from water.

We must remember that the motivation or intent in fasting is to humble oneself before God. Fasting that is sincere is a humbling of our souls before God. God noticed one of the most wicked kings, who humbled himself. Not that a man can earn anything from God, but fasting certainly catches the omniscient eye of God when a man or woman humbles himself with fasting (not to mention the coarse sackcloth that outwardly afflicted the body).

God noted the normal fast conducted by an exceedingly sinful man who fasted in sackcloth. God asked Elijah the prophet, "Have you seen how Ahab humbled himself before me" (1 Kings 21:29, ESV)? How do you think God perceives His sons and daughters, washed in the blood of Jesus and declared righteous in His sight, when they humble themselves, fast, and pray to Him?

The Absolute Fast (No Food and No Liquids)

The natural absolute fast could range from one day to three days. The shortness does not diminish the importance of the fast. The shortness magnifies the critical situation. To extend an absolute fast of more than three days would harm the physical body. Arthur Wallis succinctly expressed the purpose of an absolute fast when he wrote, "The absolute fast is an exceptional measure for an exceptional situation."[12]

The Bible provides examples of absolute fasts in both the natural and supernatural realms. The Book of Esther records a situation of

DAY 1

life or death. The Jewish people faced the threat of extermination because of the nefarious and immoral plotting of Haman, who despised Mordecai and the Jews. Queen Esther, a Jew, asked Mordecai to have all the Jews in Susa hold a fast for three days and three nights, abstaining from food and drink before she attempted to appear before the king and make a request of him, a request which could cost her life (Esther 4:15-16). She and the young women in her court would do the same (Esther 4:16). This was an absolute fast. Their fasting and prayer resulted in rescuing the Jews from imminent death, as well as the deaths of 75,000 enemies and the deaths of Haman and his ten sons.

Earlier, we discovered Ezra observed a three-day normal fast. He also observed an absolute fast for an entire day. He went into the Temple precincts and spent a night "neither eating bread nor drinking water, for he was mourning over the faithlessness of the exiles" (Ezra 10:6, ESV). The faithlessness of the exiles is a reference to Jewish men marrying foreign women.

The book of Jonah mentions one more absolute fast. The king of Nineveh, upon hearing God's impending judgment on Nineveh, abandoned his throne and covered himself with ashes. He then commanded the people of Nineveh to cover themselves and their beasts with sackcloth, refrain from eating or drinking water, and turn from their evil ways and the violence in their hands. God noted their humility and repentance and refrained from destroying them (Jonah 3:5-10). Most scholars assume this fast lasted three days. Animals and men, because they abstained from water, may have fasted from morning to evening each day. The people of Nineveh and the animals fasted and did not drink, which showed how severe the coming judgment was. Can you imagine hearing the bellowing of cattle and other animals all day long?

An example of an absolute fast in the life of Saul of Tarsus is recorded in the Book of Acts of the New Testament. Luke writes, "And for three days he was without sight and neither ate nor drank" (Acts 9:9, ESV). Saul experienced a dynamic spiritual revelation of Christ that would alter his life. God healed him of his blindness, filled him with the Spirit, and he became an apostle of Christ. He then preached the message of salvation to the Jews and the Greeks.

I recall an occasion fifty-seven years ago when I was a 16-year-old boy. The pastor of our church was facing a serious situation and asked the congregation to fast and pray for him for three days (without food or water). I agreed to his request. This is the only time in my life that I have ever done such a fast. The one aspect of this fast I remember is that I was so thirsty. My mouth felt as dry as cotton. I discovered what it was to have a coating on my tongue because of my body beginning to rid itself of toxins that had built up in my body.

Jentezen Franklin, commenting on the absolute fast, wrote, "... An absolute fast is extreme and should be done only for very short periods of time."[13] Esther's absolute fast was during a time of crisis, and called for such extreme fasting. Before entering such a rigorous fast (for no more than three days), it would be wise to consult one's family doctor if there are any questions concerning one's health. According to *Medical News Today*, abstaining from water for more than three days can cause altered mental status, kidney failure, shock liver, lactic acidosis, low blood pressure, and death.[14]

It is necessary to note why water is so important. If you undertake a 3-day fast without water because of a severe crisis or great burden on your heart for a specific need, I strongly encourage you to drink lots of water after the fast. Why? It is because water serves as a great means of ridding harmful toxins from your body. Jentezen Franklin, commenting on the importance of drinking plenty of water, wrote:

> Water is the great flushing agent in fasting. One of the signs that these toxins and poisons are being eliminated can be seen by the concentrations of toxins in our urine. These toxins may be ten times higher than normal when you're fasting. The urine turns darker because of disease-causing poison and toxins locked in your body because of terrible diets begin to be washed out.[15]

The Partial Fast (Certain Foods and Liquids Selected)

The Bible mentions this type of fasting in Daniel 10:2-3. "In those days, I, Daniel, was mourning for three weeks. I ate no delicacies, no meat or wine entered my mouth, nor did I anoint myself at all for the full three weeks." The unveiling of the vision accompanied this fast given to Daniel by an angel and the subsequent spiritual victory over the powerful kingdom of darkness. The partial fast could designate certain periods for refraining from food. Some doctors instruct their patients to avoid eating or drinking after midnight when preparing for a medical procedure and to continue this until the operation is over.

The same mindset might apply to refraining from eating breakfast and not drinking anything until noon. The partial fast could involve eating bread and drinking water for a day, or eating bread and drinking water (or juice) for breakfast and resuming normal eating the rest of the day. During that period, one would allocate time for prayer and Bible reading.

The partial fast could also be to abstain from certain foods (such as meats and sweets) for a designated period (Daniel 1:12). People often refer to this type of fast as a Daniel fast. In Daniel chapter one, Daniel, Hananiah, Mishael, and Azariah resolved not to defile themselves by eating the king's food or drinking the king's wine, but instead resolved to eat vegetables and water for ten days.

After receiving a revelation from God concerning the future of the nation of Israel, Daniel purposed in his heart to fast by abstaining from meat and sweets (delicacies) for twenty-one days. His fast demonstrated the humbling of his heart, and his seeking God led to the unfolding of the revelation and victory over powerful and sinister forces of evil (Daniel 10).

Christians find this fast convenient when engaged in a heavy workload. The restriction of their diet gives them the needed strength and energy (along with prayer and the Word of God) to engage in spiritual warfare. This fast allows for a great variation in one's diet. For example, it could be bread and water, fish, nutritious shakes, fruits, or vegetables.

Nehemiah questioned Hananiah about the condition of Judah and the Jewish remnant who had returned from captivity. Upon

DAY 1

learning that the captives were in distress and disgrace and that the wall of Jerusalem was in ruins, he sat down, wept, mourned, fasted, and prayed for several days. Although we are not told how long his fasting, mourning, and praying lasted, we know that his conversation with the king followed these humble actions. King Artaxerxes granted his request to go to Jerusalem, provided military support, and paid for building supplies (Nehemiah chapters 1-2). It is unclear what type of fasting Nehemiah practiced, as there is no mention of abstaining from water; thus, his fast may have been a partial fast.

The partial fast (abstaining from certain foods) could be associated with John the Baptist. The Bible describes John the Baptist as a forerunner of Christ. He was a man clothed in camel hair, who wore a leather belt around his waist, and ate locusts and wild honey (Mark 1:6, ESV).

The partial fast is not without self-discipline. However, this is a fast that allows some flexibility while attempting to navigate a busy schedule.

The Supernatural Fast (Fasting without food or water for 40 days)

As we stated concerning the absolute fast, a fast without food or water, the supernatural fast is the same. However, the supernatural fast has a longer timeline than the natural three days without food or water. Ordinarily, if the body goes a long time without water (for example 10 days), it will most certainly die. However, if you read Exodus 24:18; 34:28; and Deuteronomy 9:9, 18, you discover Moses did a forty-day back-to-back absolute fast, which would be supernatural. And if there were no break between his fasts, then it would be a fast of 80 days with no water, which no man could withstand. In his book, *God's Chosen Fast,* Arthur Wallis stated that Moses's two fasts were "undertaken virtually without intermission and taken together constitute what is certainly the longest fast in the Bible."[16] Whether they were back-to-back or separate, a forty-day fast without water or an 80-day fast without water would be supernatural.

I am not saying a person in the 21st century could not do a supernatural fast, but one thing is for sure: a person would have supernaturally accomplished such a feat or be dead! A wise person would never attempt such a fast! If there were a time to adhere to the Scriptures, then this would be the time. The Apostle John wrote, "Beloved, do not believe every spirit, but test the spirits to see whether they are from God, for many false prophets have gone out into the world" (I John 4:1, ESV).

The Rotational Fast.

Before writing this book, I had never heard of such a fast. However, in his book, *Fasting for Spiritual Breakthrough,* Elmer L. Towns stated, "A rotational fast consists of eating or omitting certain families of foods for designated periods. For example, someone can eat grains only every fourth day. Rotating the various food families ensures some food is available each day.[16]

DAY 2
THE POSITIONING OF THE HEART

"When thou saidst, Seek ye my face; my heart said unto thee, Thy face, LORD, will I seek."
PSALM 27:8, KJV

Seeking Christ in every thought and following Him with all your heart requires that we align our mind and desires with His.
ULISSES SOARES

In Christian circles today, some churches begin each new year by emphasizing 21 days of fasting and prayer. Such seasons of prayer and fasting have brought great blessings. There is something powerful when the body of Christ comes together corporately to fast and pray. The Bible well documents the custom of fasting, in which people abstain from food and drink to draw closer to God. There are no special blessings associated with a "specific length of time" of fasting and prayer. Whatever period one sets aside is not significant, but the act is very significant because fasting serves as a vital means of humbling our hearts before God. David wrote, "I humbled myself with fasting" (Psalm 35:13).

Fasting plays an important role in prayer. Daniel was concerned about his people (Israel) and felt troubled in his spirit. He focused his time and effort on seeking God. One of the great characteristics of Daniel was that he was great at positioning his heart towards seeking God. Even when he discovered the edict that Darius had signed prohibited praying (making a petition to any god), "He got down on his knees three times a day and prayed and gave thanks to God as he had done previously" (Daniel 6:10, ESV). While I was a student at Bible College, my professor, Walter H. Beuttler, wrote:

> Fasting in conjunction with prayer during a time of crisis or any deep need is a very effective complement to prayer in that fasting becomes synonymous with the sense of need, evidences a great earnestness, reinforces petition, intensifies desire, sharpens determination, silently continues to articulate the cry of the soul, helps to maintain an inner state of prayer and posture toward God even while attention must be given to necessary duties, assists concentration, reduces the danger of diversion through distraction and preoccupation with competing interests and strengthens the will to a continuation of the effort until the consummation of its purpose which Satan will likely seek to prevent, especially if he regards the prayer effort as being inimical to the interest of his kingdom.[17]

This attitude of the heart connected to fasting and prayer is also evident in Daniel's life with the phrase, "Then I set my face toward

DAY 2

the Lord to make request by supplications, with fasting, sackcloth, and ashes." (Daniel 9:3, NKJV). As you focus on 21 days of prayer and fasting, positioning your heart will necessitate a "setting of your face" i.e. a persistence, a wholeheartedness, an inflexible determination, a dogged perseverance in the face of many obstacles, and patient endurance while firmly believing that "God is a rewarder of those who diligently seek Him" (Hebrews 11:6).

In other words, your heart is resolute in praying and fasting for 21 days, and nothing is going to hinder or deter you from doing so. Andrew Murray wrote, "Fasting helps to express, to deepen, and to confirm the resolution that we are ready to sacrifice anything, even ourselves, to attain the Kingdom of God."[18]

Positioning your heart for the 21-day journey may necessitate saying no to competing interests to say yes to the designated time of prayer. It will require you to recognize that you have entered a spiritual wrestling match, and you will be tempted to break your fast or be sidetracked by other activities. Satan will seek to thwart your decision to fast and pray by offering suggestions to break your fast. He will tempt you with food or certain types of food you have decided to avoid. He loves to use accusations, confusion, fear, discouragement, and doubt. Your watchwords during the 21 days of prayer and fasting is, "Be sober-minded, be watchful. Your adversary the devil, prowls around like a roaring lion seeking someone to devour" (I Peter 5:8, ESV).

In some cases, fasting may be easier than praying. If you are fasting without positioning your heart for prayer, you are simply experiencing hunger without experiencing God. We could say this of the Pharisees in Christ's day, who fasted to be seen of men, thus performing a merely external religious act. Jentezen Franklin wrote that fasting without praying is dieting. He dogmatically stated, "You should not fast to lose weight, although weight loss is a normal side effect. Unless you put prayer with your fasting, there is no need to fast."[19]

Most theologians, pastors, evangelists, apostles, prophets, and mature saints of God would concur that fasting without prayer is an activity of futility. However, fasting tethered together with prayer gives the forward-moving Christian a powerful spiritual ability. Mountains are moved, strongholds are demolished, souls are converted, needs are supernaturally supplied, bodies are healed, demons are cast out, and the spiritual truth of God's Word becomes a living reality.

Dr. Billy Graham frequently linked prayer and fasting as complementary practices, emphasizing that they should be undertaken together to achieve great spiritual fruit.

Positioning your heart is refusing to yield to your feelings. Jesus did not say, "If you feel like praying" or "If you feel like fasting," but "When you pray," and "When you fast" (Matthew 6:5-7, 6:16-17).

Positioning your heart requires you to pray before God with a broken and humble heart. God revealed why He chose David over King Saul when He said, "I have found David, the son of Jesse, a man after my own heart, who will do all My will" (Acts 13:22, NKJV).

Samuel discovered this truth when God told Samuel that men look on the outward appearance, but "God looks on the heart." God

DAY 2

looked at David's heart. God certainly saw the ability David possessed. More importantly, God saw David's humble heart.

Jesus told a parable of a Pharisee and a tax collector. The Pharisee and the tax collector were both praying in the temple. The Pharisee prayed, "God, I thank You that I am not like other men—extortioners, unjust, adulterers or even as this tax collector. I fast twice a week; I give tithes of all that I possess" (Luke 18:11, NKJV). The tax collector, beating his breast, prayed, God, be merciful to me a sinner" (Luke 18:13, NKJV)!

The tax collector went to his home justified rather than the Pharisee. Jesus gave the reason for the tax collector's justification. The reason for the tax collector's justification was also the purpose of the parable. He said, "For everyone who exalts himself will be humbled, and he who humbles himself will be exalted" (Luke 18:14, NKJV).

DAY 3
THE OPENING OF OUR EYES

"And he was three days without sight and neither ate nor drank."
ACTS 9:9, NKJV

"Revelation does not mean man finding God, but God finding man, God sharing His secrets with us, God showing us Himself. In revelation, God is the agent as well as the object."
-J. L. PACKER

Have you ever wondered what Saul of Tarsus was thinking for three days as he tarried in Damascus, blind, hungry, and thirsty? Saul had just experienced a supernatural conversion while en route to Damascus, where he sought to persecute the church. He saw a light from heaven around him, and when he fell on the ground, he heard the risen Lord Jesus Christ calling out his name and questioning his egregious acts of persecution. Addressing Jesus as Lord of his life, and being blind, he was escorted by the men who had journeyed with him to Damascus.

At Damascus, we see Saul conducting an absolute fast (abstaining from food and water) and praying. Ananias is informed by the Lord that Saul was in the vicinity of the street called Straight and that he was praying. Ananias, finding Saul, stated that the Lord Jesus, who had appeared to Saul on the road to Damascus so that he might receive his sight and be filled with the Holy Spirit had sent him. For three days, Saul's world had been filled with darkness. During this time, Saul's spiritual eyes were being opened before the opening of his physical eyes. Robert Tourville wrote that the three days of prayer and fasting "gave the persecutor time to consider his past".[20] Tourville stated that Paul, in his epistles, spoke of being dead in trespasses and sins and thinks of all he did as works of darkness (Romans 13:12; Ephesians 5:11).[21] One of Paul's prayers for the church of Ephesus was that the "God of our Lord Jesus Christ the Father of Glory, may give unto you the spirit of wisdom and revelation in the knowledge of him" (Ephesians 1:17, KJV).

It is interesting that, although Saul was without sight for three days, he saw a vision. He did not see the vision with his natural eyes. It was not external vision; it was internal. It was supernatural. Ananias was a disciple of Jesus Christ who lived in Damascus. "The Lord called to him in a vision, Ananias (Acts 9:10, NIV)! We have a man with sight, seeing a vision (Ananias), and a man without sight (Saul), also seeing a vision. The Greek word for vision is *horasis* (#3706) and according to Strong, it means, "The act of gazing at, external and internal as an inspired appearance, Supernatural sight."[22]

Jesus told a story about the rich man and Lazarus, a beggar. Both died, and both were buried. Both had a soul. Lazarus' soul was car-

DAY 3

ried to Abraham's bosom, and the rich man's soul went to hell. In hell, he lifted his eyes, looked, and saw Abraham far away and Lazarus at his side. The soul has the spiritual capacity to see supernaturally. The soul has the spiritual capacity to know God. Fasting and prayer help us see spiritual truths and things we have never seen. God can illumine our hearts and give us spiritual visions, should He in His sovereign will so desire to do so. Such visions would never contradict or supersede the Word of God.

In 2 Kings 13-17, we find the story of an invading army of the king of Syria surrounding the prophet Elisha in a place called Dothan. Elisha's servant arose early in the morning and suddenly noticed an army of horses and chariots surrounding the city of Dothan. The servant was afraid and cried out to Elisha, "Oh, master, what shall we do?" Elisha responded, "Don't worry about it—there are more on our side than on their side." Notice the following words: "And Elisha prayed."

How awesome is the power of prayer! You do not have to worry about the circumstances surrounding your life, no matter how disconcerting they may be. You are united with others who are fasting and praying with you. Rather than resorting to fear, pray! Elijah prayed for spiritual revelation, saying, "Lord, I pray, open his eyes that he may see." Unlike Saul of Tarsus, the servant was not physically blind. Yet, like Saul, who received a spiritual revelation, this servant needed a spiritual revelation. God opened the eyes of the young man, and he saw the mountain full of horses and chariots of fire all around Elijah. He realized that although he was in a physical battle, he could fix his eyes on that which was unseen. We must learn that our battles are not with flesh and blood but against spiritual wickedness and rulers of darkness in the heavenly realm.

The time you set aside for 21 days of prayer and fasting may be a time that the Lord may open your spiritual eyes and understanding. He may reveal the Word of God to your hungry and thirsting heart. It may be a preparatory time before God sovereignly and supernaturally works in your life. It may be a time in which "The eyes of your understanding being enlightened; that ye may know what is the hope of his calling, and what the riches of the glory of his inheritance in the saints" (Ephesians 1:8, KJV). Fasting may be a time that Christ challenges your spiritual lukewarmness, exhorting you to "anoint your eyes with eye salve, that you may see" (Revelation 3:18, KJV).

THE DENYING OF OUR FLESH

"Is this the fast I have chosen, a day for a man to afflict his soul..."
ISAIAH 58:5, KJV

"Self-will and the rule of the stomach screamed during the fast, often creating irritability and anger. Fasting is where I can reveal the battlefield within myself, crucified, all rights to self, and seek God's healing from my selfishness."[23]
- OSWALD CHAMBERS

Our fleshly appetites and desires reign sovereignly as king over our lives until they are subdued by faith in the powerful working of the Holy Spirit. Different translations of this verse speak of "denying our flesh," "afflicting our soul," or "humbling himself." When we fast, we are taking time to deprive ourselves for spiritual purposes. We are saying to our old nature, "No," and we do so to say, "Yes," to our Heavenly Father. Jesus understood the principle of self-denial and made it a condition for following him. Jesus said, "If any man will come after me, let him first deny himself and take up his cross and follow me" (Matthew 16:24, KJV). But self-denial is not part of the philosophical concept of our society. It runs contrary to the culture.

Paul acknowledged the potential power of the Holy Spirit to work in us when he prayed, "Now to Him who is able to do exceedingly abundantly above all we ask or think, according to the power that works in us." (Ephesians 4:20, NKJV).

C.S. Lewis wrote, "Fasting asserts the will against the appetite - the reward being self-mastery and the danger pride: involuntary hunger subjects appetites and will together to the Divine will, furnishing an occasion for submission and exposing us to the danger of rebellion. But the redemptive effect of suffering lies chiefly in its tendency to reduce the rebel will."[24]

During the 21 days of fasting and prayer, as we submit our bodies to the discipline of fasting and prayer, we must remind ourselves that fasting is not a meritorious act. It is, as we stated earlier, "a humbling of our soul." Denying our flesh is never easy.

Let me encourage you to read the Word of God, deny yourself, and yield to what God is speaking to you through God's Word and by the Holy Spirit during these 21 days of prayer and fasting. God's Word contains both a sweet message and a bitter message. The prophet Jeremiah felt dejected, knowing about the future destruction of Jerusalem and the captivity of his people (Jeremiah 15). Yet he proclaimed, "Your words were found, and I ate them, and your words became to me a joy and the delight of my heart" (Jeremiah 15:16).

DAY 4

John wrote, "Then the voice which I heard from heaven spoke to me again and said, 'Go take the little book which is open in the hand of the angel who stands on the sea and on the earth.' So I went to the angel and said to him, 'Give me the little book.' And he said to me, 'Take and eat it; and it will make your stomach bitter, but it will be sweet as honey in your mouth (Revelation 10:8-9, NKJV).'"

Incorporating the Word of God in our lives concerning fasting is not easy. But the spiritual results are quite edifying (sweet), especially when we see the work that the Holy Spirit has done in our hearts and lives during the 21 days of praying and fasting.

If we are not careful, we can take pride in the fact that we fasted for three whole weeks. Fasting is never to impress God, to impress others, or to impress ourselves. Andrew Murray wrote, "Prayer is the one hand with which we grasp the invisible; fasting, the other, with which we let loose and cast away the visible."[25] When we fast, we allow our spirit to become more powerful than our flesh. When we deny our flesh (body) of natural food, we empower our spirit to be empowered by God's Spirit. Billy Graham said, "Fasting is surrender in action. It is giving up what satisfies the flesh in exchange for what nourishes."[26]

The Apostle Paul declared, "I have been crucified with Christ, and I no longer live, but Christ lives in me. The life I now live in the body, I live by the faith in the Son of God who loved me and gave himself for me" (Galatians 2:20, NIV). Fasting acknowledges that as Christians, we have been crucified with Christ, and this knowledge assists us in practically experiencing the crucifixion of the flesh.

When Christ died, I died. When Paul declared he was crucified with Christ, he declared that his old sinful nature was crucified when Christ died on the cross of Calvary. He was identifying with Christ and applying the efficacy of Christ's death. We can be triumphant over our sinful, selfish nature as we understand that our sinful, selfish nature is not dead, but we are dead to it. It is no longer I, but Christ that lives in me!

The crucified life is also characterized in Paul's statement, "For the love of God controls us, because we have concluded this: that one has died for all, therefore all have died; and he died for all, that those who live might no longer live for themselves but for him who for their sake died and was raised" (2 Corinthians 5:14-15, ESV). Arthur Wallis wisely wrote, "The cross must work in us if the life is to be centered in God."[27]

A.W. Tozer, in his book entitled *The Crucified Life*, wrote, "What I mean by 'the crucified life' is a life who given over to the Lord in absolute humility and obedience: a sacrifice pleasing to the Lord." He further stated, "Being dead and yet alive is one of the strange inconsistencies of the life established for us by Jesus' dying on the cross. But oh, the blessedness of these seeming inconsistencies."[28]

When we deny ourselves through fasting, we embrace the tension between arduous discipline and joyful delight, the physical pain of hunger and the purposeful pain of self-denial, the cry of the flesh and the inarticulate cry of the soul, joyfully finding God and yet desperately pursuing Him.

When we deny ourselves, it is a way of disciplining our physical bodies. We refuse to be dictated to or preoccupied with our fleshly

DAY 4

appetites. It is also a practice in which we afflict our souls or humble our souls before God. One of the great benefits of self-denial is that we become laser-focused on doing the things that God desires us to do.

"When we crucify ourselves, we live by a new value system. We give up our inner compulsions for self-power, self-protection, self-success, and gathering 'stuff.' We give everything to God for His control."[29]

DAY 5: THE FAITH OF A MUSTARD SEED: QUANTITY OR QUALITY?

"So Jesus said to them, Because of your unbelief; for assuredly, I say to you, if you have faith as a mustard seed you will say to this mountain, 'Move from here to there,' and it will move: and nothing will be impossible for you."

MATTHEW 17:20, NKJV

"No faith is required to do the possible; actually only a morsel of this atom power stuff is needed to do the impossible, for a piece as large as a mustard seed will do more than we ever dreamed of."

- LEONARD RAVENHILL

Jesus was confronted by the father whose son was demon-possessed and had tried to commit suicide on many occasions. The father had taken his son to the disciples of Jesus, looking for a cure. But he was disappointed. The disciples could not cast out the demon of the boy. So, the father took his son to Jesus and explained what had happened. Notice the words of Jesus. "O unbelieving and perverse generation," Jesus replied, "How long shall I stay with you? How long shall I put up with you? Bring the boy here to me." Jesus rebuked the demon, and it came out of the boy, and he was healed at that moment" (Matthew 17:17-18, NIV).

The disciples of Christ were perplexed because, in the past, they had cast out demons by the authority of Christ given to them. So, they went to Jesus and asked him why they were unsuccessful. Jesus gave them the reason why they could not cast out the demon from the boy. He said, "Because you have so little faith. Truly I tell you, if you have faith as small as a mustard seed, you can say to this mountain, 'Move from here to there' and it will move. Nothing will be impossible for you" (Matthew 17:17-21, NIV).

What is known about the mustard seed? In 1857, Francis Bacon wrote about the mustard seed, describing how it could withstand cold and heat and was resilient enough to return year after year without dying like other seeds.[30] A mustard seed has a diameter of 1 millimeter.[31] "The mustard seed Christ referred to may have been 'the *Salvadora perisica*'. It can grow to twenty feet wide and tall. They can thrive in environments typically hostile to plants. Their seeds are very small, but they grow large."[32]

Rhodus, commenting on the phrase "faith as a mustard seed," emphasized the word "as" and felt the emphasis should be placed on the character of the mustard seed.[33] He believed that Jesus was not looking for little faith but strong character of faith.[34] It is not about the quantity of faith, but the quality of it. This reflects a small amount of faith compared to a small amount of faith that is accompanied by

DAY 5

fasting—humbling the soul before God. It is faith that is accompanied by fasting and prayer.

Although Matthew 17:21 is omitted in many reliable manuscripts, Mark 9:29 includes the phrase "prayer and fasting" (KJV). The Pulpit Commentary clarifies Matthew 17:21, which refers to "fasting and prayer," to expel certain types of demons.

Though all things are possible to faith, some works are more difficult of accomplishment than others. *This kind* can mean only this kind of evil spirit, or demons generally exercised successfully their power over devils with special prayer or fasting. The words point to a truth in the spiritual world, that there are different degrees in the Satanic hierarchy (compare Ch. xii. 45); some demons are more malignant than others and have greater power over the souls of men. In the present case, the possession was of long standing; it involved a bodily malady: it was of an intense and unusual character. The mere word exorcism, or the name of Jesus, spoken with little spiritual faith, could not overcome the mighty enemy. The exorcist needed special preparation; he must inspire and augment his faith by prayer and self-discipline. Prayer invokes the aid of God and puts one's self unreservedly in his hands; fasting subdues the flesh, arouses the soul's energies brings into exercise the higher parts of man's nature. Thus equipped, a man is open to receive power from on high, and can quell the assaults of the evil one.[35]

DAY 6
HUNGRY, AND HUNGERING FOR THE WORD OF GOD

"Behold, I long for Your precepts; in Your righteousness give me life."
PSALM 119:40, ESV

"The soul can do without everything except the word of God, without which none at all of its wants are provided for."
-CHARLES SPURGEON

In the Gospel of Matthew, we find Jesus had fasted for forty days and forty nights and afterward was hungry. Satan appeared and tempted him, saying, "If you are the Son of God, command that these stones become bread" (Matthew 4:3, NKJV). But Jesus answered and said, "It is written, 'Man shall not live by bread alone, but by every word that proceeds from the mouth of God'" (Matthew 4:4, NKJV).

Jesus quoted from Deuteronomy 8:3. Although he was physically hungry, he was spiritually full of the Word of God. He countered all of Satan's temptations one by one, referencing the Word of God.

Like David, Jesus had hidden the Word of God in his heart, but, unlike David, the Son of David was sinless. The writer of the book of Hebrews wrote, "For we do not have a high priest who is unable to empathize with our weaknesses, but we have one who has been tempted in every way, just as we are—yet he did not sin" (Hebrews 4:15, NIV).

Job, amid the trial of his faith, declared, "I have treasured the words of His mouth More than my necessary food." (Job 23:12, NKJV). When fasting and praying for 21 days, you may find the Word of God, "sweeter than the honey and the honeycomb" (Psalm 19:10, KJV).

Do you recall the story when Saul's troops were distressed because Saul had placed the people under oath, saying, "Cursed is the man who eats any food until evening, before I have taken vengeance on my enemies" (1 Samuel 14:24, NKJV). Saul was essentially saying, "No one eats until the battle is won." Samuel wrote, "Now all the people of the land came to a forest; and there was honey on the ground. And when the people had come into the woods, there was the honey dripping; but no one put his hand to their mouth, for the people feared the oath" (1 Samuel 14:25, NKJV).

However, Saul's son Jonathan had not heard about his father's command to the people. Feeling hungry, he saw the honey, took the rod in his hand, and dipped it into the honeycomb. An immediate physical effect occurred when he ate the honey: "His countenance brightened" (1 Samuel 14:27, NKJV). The people then informed Jonathan of his father's oath. Still, Jonathan stood firm and remarked

DAY 6

that his father had troubled the land. He declared, "Look now, how my countenance has brightened because I tasted a little of this honey" (1 Samuel 14:29, NKJV).

David wrote, "How sweet are Your words to my taste, sweeter than honey to my mouth" (Psalm 119:103, NKJV). Friend, when fasting and praying for 21 days, when you are hungry, you can find spiritual strength and nourishment "eating" the Word of God! Jesus found spiritual strength in the Word (overcoming the temptations of Satan). Job found spiritual sustenance in the Word (overcoming his trials). Jeremiah was called to share the word of God with the nation of Israel. His message of condemnation was bitter, and he suffered persecution, but he said, "Your words were found, and I ate them, And your word was to me the joy and the rejoicing of my heart of my heart" (Jeremiah 15:16, NKJV).

When Jesus fasted for forty days, he experienced hunger. He endured hunger pangs- those uncomfortable sensations of the intestines contracting or churning in response to, or we might say, acknowledging the absence of food. He is the great High Priest "who is touched with the feelings of our infirmities" (Hebrews 4:15, KJV). When exhausted, hungry, and tempted by Satan, the Word of God flowed from his lips effortlessly and with authority as he rebuked the tempter, saying, "Man shall not live by bread alone, but by every word that proceedeth out of the mouth of God" (Matthew 4:4, KJV).

Richard Foster understood the spiritual enrichment and sustenance that comes "by every word that comes from the mouth of God." (Matthew 4:4, ESV) He wrote, "...Therefore, in experiences of fasting, we are not so much abstaining from food as we are feasting on the word of God. Fasting is feasting!"[36]

The point Jesus endeavored to make is that in every trial and temptation of life, our trust is not in the physically tangible. Our trust is in God, who is eternal. Just as Israel's journey in the desert necessitated trusting the eternal God each morning to supply manna (by just speaking a word from His mouth), we trust in Him, the Living Word, and His written Word.

"We are feeding on God and, just like the Israelites who were sustained in the wilderness by the miraculous manna from heaven, so we are sustained by the Word of God."[37]

Regardless of the type of fast you choose to do during the 21 days of corporate prayer and fasting, I encourage you to read the Word, meditate on the Word of God, and memorize the Word of God. How awesome would it be to have spiritual hunger pangs for the Word of God!?

In Psalm 119, the author glorifies God and magnifies and esteems the Word of God. We quickly note how the author of the Psalm hungered for and valued the Word of God. Let your time of fasting be a delightful time of feasting on the Word of God.

Here are some verses of the Psalm in which the author valued and delighted in the Word.

- Your Word have I hidden in my heart that I might not sin against You. V. 11.
- I will delight myself in Your statutes; I will not forget Your word. V. 16.

DAY 6

- Your testimonies also are my delight and my counselors. V. 24.
- I will run the course of Your commandments, for You shall enlarge my heart. V. 32.
- I will delight myself in Your commandments, which I love. V. 47.
- I will never forget Your precepts, for by them You have given me life. V. 93.
- Oh, how I love Your law! It is my meditation all the day. V. 97.
- Your testimonies I have taken as a heritage forever, for they are the rejoicing of my heart. V. 111.
- Therefore I love Your commandments more than gold, yes, than fine gold! V. 127.
- I opened my mouth and panted, for I longed for Your commandments. V. 131.
- Thy word is very pure: Therefore thy servant loves it. V. 140.
- My eyes are awake through the night watches, That I may meditate in Your word. V. 148.
- My soul keeps Your testimonies, and I love them exceedingly. V. 167.
- I long for Thy salvation, O Lord, and Your law is my delight. V. 174.

Scriptures are taken from the NKJV.

DAY 7
SINCERELY SEEKING GOD

"You will seek me and find me, when you seek me with all your heart."
JEREMIAH 29:13, KJV

"The evil habit of seeking 'God-and' effectively prevents us from finding God in full revelation."
-A. W. TOZER

The nation of Israel was heading into the Babylonian Captivity, which would last seventy years. However, if they would call upon the Lord and seek Him earnestly, they would discover that God really did have thoughts of peace and not of evil, and that He truly wanted to give them a future and a hope.

In our text, the word "seek" appears twice. It is interesting to note that the Hebrew language used two different words for "seek." The first reference to "seek" is the Hebrew word *darash*, which can mean "to inquire, search carefully, or investigate."[38] The second reference to "seek" in our text is the Hebrew word *Baqash,* which, according to Strong's Concordance, "has a stronger sense of actively pursuing something with the intention of finding it or obtaining it".[39] The New King James Version translates our text, "And you will **seek** Me and find Me, when you **search** for Me with all your heart."

Fasting facilitates the endeavor to seek God with all your heart. Seeking God with all your heart means that your heart is void of divisive and competing interests. It is a total abandonment of subtle idolatries that have relegated God to a secondary position and prioritized the cares of the world, the deceitfulness of riches, and the lust for other things over him. Andrew Murray wrote, "Because of the negative effects of the body upon the spirit *prayer needs fasting* for its full growth. Prayer is the one hand with which we grasp the invisible. Fasting is the other hand with which we let go of the visible."[40]

Seeking God with a whole heart is characterized by importunity. It is seeking God patiently and confidently with insistent persistence while believing the promise of God. Such persistence continues to ask, continues to seek, and continues to knock until the door is opened (see Luke 11:9).

It rests not only on the promise of God but also on the character of God, who cannot lie. God will always respond to those who seek Him. Isaiah wrote, "I have not spoken in secret, from somewhere in a land of darkness; I have not said to Jacob's descendants, 'Seek me in vain.' I the Lord, speak truth; I declare what is right" (Isaiah 45:19, NIV). And Jesus assured the seeking heart of an answer. He stated, "For everyone who asks receives, and the one who seeks finds, and the one who knocks it will be opened" (Luke 11:10, ESV).

DAY 7

We see how King David diligently sought after God after his adultery with Bathsheba had been exposed by Nathan the prophet. Nathan declared to David, "The Lord has put away your sin; you shall not die. Nevertheless, because of this deed you have utterly scorned the Lord, the child who is born to you shall die" (2 Samuel 12:13-14, NKJV). The baby became severely ill. For six days, David fasted and lay all night on the ground. On the seventh day, the child died.

Who can truly understand the agony and heartbreak that both David and Bathsheba experienced? Although David's fasting and seeking God did not lead to God sparing his son's life, it illustrates a deep sense of brokenness, sincerity, and wholeheartedness in seeking God. We should take note of that. It also reinforces the fact that fasting and prayer are intricately bound together to achieve the main objective.

David was informed that the child was dead. "Then David arose from the earth and washed and anointed himself and changed his clothes. And he went into the house of the Lord and worshipped. He then went into his own house. And when he asked, they set food before him, and he ate" (2 Samuel 12:20, ESV).

His behavior puzzled his servants. They inquired of David concerning the matter. David responded to their inquiry, "While the child was still alive. I fasted and wept, for I said, 'Who knows whether the Lord will be gracious to me, that the child may live?' But now he is dead. Why should I fast? Can I bring him back again? I shall go to him, but he will not return to me" (2 Samuel 22-23, ESV).

DAY 8
WORSHIPPING AND FASTING

"While they were worshiping the Lord and fasting, the Holy Spirit said, 'Set apart for me Barnabas and Saul for the work to which I have called them.'"

ACTS 13:2, NIV

"And fasting is chiefly an aid to prayer, so much so, that it has frequently been found a means, in the hand of God, of confirming and increasing, not one virtue, but also seriousness of spirit, sincerity, sensitivity and tenderness of conscience, deadness to the world, and consequently a love of God, and of every holy and heavenly feeling."

- JOHN WESLEY

This verse is very interesting. The King James Version reads, "As they ministered to the Lord and fasted, the Holy Ghost said, Separate me Barnabas and Saul for the work whereunto I have called them." The New American Standard Bible states that while they were "ministering."

The year is A.D. 48. It had been 18 years since the Holy Spirit was poured out on the Day of Pentecost. It had been 15 years since Paul had been converted and received a call to minister to the Gentiles. The gospel had not been taken into all the world. The early church had been indolent. It is at this time that God, who loves broken humanity and yearns for their salvation, initiates a great outreach for a great harvest among the Gentiles in Asia Minor and Europe.

Jesus had declared that after the disciples received the outpouring of the Holy Spirit, they would be His witnesses in Jerusalem, Judea, Samaria, and the remote parts of the world.

Until 48 A.D., minimal effort had been made to reach the Gentiles with the Gospel. Cornelius and his household had been converted, and Paul, Barnabas, Simeon, Lucius, and Manaen were **ministering** to the Gentiles in Antioch, but God had a greater plan.

From the midst of these five men who were ministering to the Lord and fasting, the Holy Spirit said, "Set apart for Me Barnabas and Saul (Paul) for the work which I have called them" (Acts 13:2, NASB). In Acts 13:3, the Greek word "set" means to "release or disperse." In his commentary on the book of Acts, Robert Tourville wrote that "Ministering and fasting are concurrent actions, i.e., while they were ministering, they were fasting; the Holy Spirit, perhaps spoke through a word of prophecy, to these five men."[41] The word of prophecy was a confirmation of Saul's call in Acts 9:15. Paul was to take the gospel to the Gentiles and take Barnabas with him.

The context of this divine intervention is that the five men were fasting. I wonder if these men had a stirring in their hearts for the

DAY 8

lost and were seeking God's guidance. We don't know, but we do know their fasting contributed to God's intervention and provided clear guidance for Paul and Barnabas in a missionary endeavor to reach Gentiles with the gospel.

In Christian circles today, we may say that the five men received a *word from the Lord*. The *word of the Lord* has several meanings. Primarily, it is a reference to the Bible, inspired by the Holy Spirit, which is our only rule of faith. It is also used to reference the gospel of Jesus Christ. And finally, as in this case, it was a word given specifically to Paul and Barnabas by the Holy Spirit, commissioning them to do missionary work. The Holy Spirit was the one who sent them forth, not the church. Note that in Acts 13:4, they were sent out by the Holy Spirit.

It was not a word that they would have found in the Old Testament. The Holy Spirit spoke and gave guidance. Such a word from the Lord never contradicts the Word of God (the Bible). Paul and Barnabas would fulfil the scripture, "But you shall receive power when the Holy Spirit has come upon you: and you shall be witnesses to Me in Jerusalem, and in all Judea and Samaria, and to the end of the earth" (Acts 1:8, NKJV). Fostered in an atmosphere of corporate fasting and prayer, it was a word spoken by the Holy Spirit that propelled a foreign missions outreach that changed the course of history. Christianity would become the dominant religion of the Roman Empire.

The Holy Spirit continues to speak today! A time set apart to pray and fast may provide God an opportunity to speak a prophetic word to your heart that offers guidance and direction. Just as the Word was a defining moment for Paul and Barnabas, so the Holy Spirit can speak to your heart. One must always remember that a word from God will never contradict God's Word. The Bible is the track on which the train of experience must ride. Knowing God's Word will protect you from anything bizarre. It will keep you from being derailed in your spiritual walk and service to the Lord.

Hudson Taylor is a great illustration of how God actively calls men and women. After his conversion at the age of 15, God impressed upon him one word: China. Concerning his calling, he wrote in his autobiography, "The impression was wrought into my soul that it was in China the Lord wanted me." It was after his conversion that his parents revealed to him that from the time he was born, they had prayed that he would be a missionary to China.

Hudson Taylor was a British Protestant missionary who served in China for 51 years and founded the China Inland Mission. As a result of his efforts, over 800 missionaries came to China, 125 schools were established, 18,000 individuals became Christians, and 300 mission stations, employing 500 local workers in addition to missionaries from other countries, were established in all of the 18 provinces of China.[42]

So, how are we to reconcile the translations of *ministering* verses with *worshiping*? Perhaps the answer is found in Paul's words: "And whatever you do, in word or deed, do everything in the name of the Lord Jesus, giving thanks to God the Father through him" (Colossians 3:17, ESV). We may also note Paul's words to the Romans:

DAY 8

"Present your bodies as a living sacrifice, holy and acceptable to God, which is your reasonable service" (Romans 12:1, KJV).

I have found that a partial fast provides enough energy to minister or worship God while accomplishing limited tasks (deeds) and enough energy to minister or worship God in prayer, praise, and singing (words). When performing limited activities (deeds), fasting becomes the inarticulate cry of the soul for God.

"She did not depart from the temple, worshipping with fasting and prayer night and day" (Acts 1:37, ESV).

Luke wrote of a prophetess named Anna. Having established her heritage as being a faithful Jew, he wrote, "She was advanced in years, having lived with her husband seven years from when she was a virgin, and then as a widow until she was eighty-four. She did not depart from the temple, worshipping with fasting and prayer night and day" (Luke 2:36-37, ESV). Note that the element of fasting is associated with worshipping and praying. Worship, prayer, and fasting formed a strong threefold cord of Anna's spiritual life. Are you willing to add fasting as a discipline in your spiritual life? Such an extraordinary form of discipline that runs contrary to cultural norms.

Having lost her husband after being married for only seven years, she decided to devote the rest of her life to being a widow. Some scholars think that Anna would have been married at age 14, lived with her husband until age 21, and lived as a widow for 84 years. Such a scenario would have made her 105 years old. Luke wrote that Anna was "advanced in years" (Luke 2:36, ESV). However, we do not know how old she was when she married.

Anna's commitment to worshiping with fasting and prayer night and day in the temple, while being at least 84 years old, is remarkable. And that she was a prophetess, looking for the redemption of Israel, shows her perpetual steadfastness and unwavering faith in the promises of God.

In Christian circles today, she would be called a "prayer warrior." She constantly attended all the stated hours of prayer. The reference to "day and night" suggests she was continually worshipping, praying, and fasting. Such deliberate devotion and longing for the Messiah was rewarded. Anna, along with Simeon, on the same glorious day, saw the Christ Child, the consolation of Israel and the redeemer of Jerusalem.

When I think about Anna's devotion, her praying and fasting, I am reminded of the story that Mark Batterson wrote in his book entitled *The Circle Maker*. It is the story of a woman named Elizabeth Dabney. Around 1925, while living in North Philly, an area known for its difficulties, she asked God to bless her husband (a preacher) with spiritual victory in the neighborhood if she committed to pray for him. She felt the Lord had assured her He would, and that He was prompting her to meet with Him the next day at the Schuylkill River at 7:30 a.m. Worried about missing her appointment with the Lord, she stayed awake all night crocheting. As she arrived at the designated spot, the presence of God overshadowed her. She drew a circle in the sand and promised God she would walk with Him day and night for three years in prayer, fasting for seventy-two hours each week for two years if God would bless her and her husband

DAY 8

with a church and a congregation in the area. God poured out blessings on them, and soon, their mission became too small, prompting her to pray until God provided a larger building.[43]

The Pentecostal Evangel published her testimony under the title "*What It Means to Pray Through*," an article that sparked a prayer movement around the world. Mrs. Dabney received three million letters from people wanting to learn how to pray through.[44] She published a book entitled *What It Means to Pray Through*.

Richard Foster, in his book *Celebration of Discipline*, wrote, "Fasting must forever centre on God. It must be God-initiated and God-ordained. Like the prophetess Anna, we need to be 'worshipping with fasting' (Luke 2:37)."[45] Commenting on Acts 13:2, he wrote, "Like that apostolic band at Antioch, 'fasting' 'worshipping the Lord' must be said in the same breath."[46]

In Christian circles, people often say, "Worship is the pathway into the presence of God." If worship is the pathway, then the discipline of fasting and praying intensifies our desire and hastens our steps on this pathway.

DAY 9
SPITTING SEEDS, PICKING BONES, AND HAVING ONION BREATH

"We remember the fish we ate in Egypt at no cost—also the cucumbers, melons, leaks, onions, and garlic. But now we have lost our appetite. We never see anything but this manna."
NUMBERS 11:5-6, KJV

And the whole congregation of the people of Israel murmured against Moses and Aaron in the wilderness, and said to them, "Would we had died by the hand of the Lord in the land of Egypt, when we sat by the fleshpots and ate bread to the full; for you have brought us out into this wilderness to kill this whole assembly with hunger."
EXODUS 16:2-3, KJV

"Gratitude and murmuring never abide in the same heart at the same time."
- E M. BOUNDS

While enslaved in Egypt, the Israelites enjoyed iconic food. Even though they were free from Egypt's bondage, their cravings still enslaved the rabble, despite God graciously providing manna from heaven. "Now the rabble that was among them had a strong craving. And the people of Israel wept once more and said, 'Oh, that we had meat to eat! We remember the fish we enjoyed in Egypt, which cost us nothing, along with the cucumbers, melons, leeks, onions, and garlic'" (Numbers 11:4-5, ESV). They reminisced about the abundance of food they had in Egypt while sitting around eating melons, spitting the seeds, eating fish and picking the bones, eating leeks and onions, and having bad breath. But they seemingly had amnesia, failing to remember their cruel bondage, cruel taskmasters, gathering straw, making bricks, and crying out to God for deliverance.

The cuisine of ancient Egypt lasted over three thousand years and retained many consistent traits until well into Greco-Roman times. The staples of both poor and wealthy Egyptians were bread and beer, often accompanied by green-shooted onions, other vegetables, and, to a lesser extent, meat, game, and fish.[47]

"Meat came from domesticated animals, game, and poultry. This possibly included partridge, quail, pigeon, ducks, and geese."[48] However, for those who could afford it, the most important animals were cattle and sheep.

The lust for food exists in all of us, just as it did with the Israelites. During times or seasons of fasting, the temptation to give in to the desire for food is noticeably magnified. When we think of the iconic foods of America, such as hotdogs, hamburgers, cheesesteaks, fried chicken, steaks, shrimp, crabs, lobster, barbeque ribs, pork chops, turkey, ham, and cuisines from other countries, we, like the Israelites may crave to sit beside our fleshpots and eat to the full. Having men-

DAY 9

tioned such iconic food, you may need to rebuke the temptation and lust for food "**NOW!**"

The prophet Samuel gave a stinging rebuke to Eli, the priest, concerning the unbridled, lustful, and indulgent acts of the sons of Eli as they received sacrificial offerings from the people. God said, "Why then do you scorn my sacrifices and offerings that I commanded for my dwelling, and honor your sons above me by fattening yourselves on the choicest parts of every offering of my people, Israel" (1 Samuel 2:29, ESV)?

Albert Barnes, commenting on Exodus 16: 2-3 wrote, "So the priests, instead of being grateful for the provision made for them, in their pampered pride became dissatisfied, wantonly broke the laws of God which regulated their share of the offerings and gave themselves up to an unbridled indulgence of their passions and their covetousness."[49] Eli was honoring his sons and dishonoring God. Eli's sons lacked control over their lustful appetites.

What are the three reasons that contribute to an excessive affection for food and hinder our physical appetite from being controlled by the spiritual discipline of fasting? The first reason is our sinful, fallen nature, which drives us to seek selfish pleasure that easily binds us to a lustful appetite. "The heart is deceitful above all things and desperately wicked, who can know it (Jeremiah 19:9, KJV)?"

The second reason is that when you intentionally choose to fast for a specific period, such as 21 days, Satan sometimes seeks to hinder you from the spiritual discipline of fasting and praying. When Jesus fasted for forty days, Satan appeared and challenged him regarding his hunger pains. The tempter urged him to use his omnipotent power to turn stones into bread.

Satan has existed for a long time, longer than humanity itself, and he has perfected his art of temptation. Generations of men, women, boys, and girls have fallen victim to his wickedly skilled machinations. Satan exploited the craving for food to diminish Adam and Eve's desire for God. The fall of Adam and Eve was a result of Satan's powerful lure. The sight of the forbidden fruit offered delight, a promised insight, and a single bite of the fruit led to their flight from Paradise.

The third reason is that man, left to himself and possessing a selfish, sinful nature, will worship or lust for something. John Piper wrote, "What masters us becomes our gods, and Paul warns us about those whose 'god is their belly'" (Philippians 3:19)."[50] Are you the master of your stomach or its slave? Dr. A.W. Tozer said, "I fast just often enough to let my stomach know who's boss."[51] There is nothing wrong with having an appetite. God wisely designed our physical body to possess an appetite to avoid the death of the body. But allowing our appetites to reign sovereign over our spirit is another side of the coin of self-preservation.

When we hear about the cities of Sodom and Gomorrah, our thoughts immediately race to their sexual sins. Still, we often overlook their lust for food as one of the contributing factors to their annihilation. "Now this was the sin of your sister Sodom: She and her daughters were arrogant, **overfed** (emphasis mine) and unconcerned, they did not help the poor and needy. They were haughty

DAY 9

and did detestable things before me. Therefore I did away with them as you have seen." (Ezekiel 16:49-51, NIV)

The fleshpots juxtapose carnal appetites with spiritual delights. God, who is infinitely good and omnipotent, was certainly capable of leading the Israelites through the wilderness. They could have written a journal full of powerful testimonies of His supernatural and superabundant provisions that preceded their speedy entrance into the promised land, a land flowing with milk and honey. But tragically, we see them reminiscing and longing for the carnal instead of the supernatural.

During the 21 days of prayer and fasting, we must continually align our hearts to experience God. God's nature is such that he wants to invade and impact your life with supernatural blessings. He longs to do good because He is good. He longs to hear your prayers and answer them. Firm assurance that He "has heard our prayers and seen our tears" prepares the way for ultimate victory.

DAY 10
DON'T FALTER, FAINT, OR FAIL!

"Let us not become weary in doing good, for at the proper time we will reap a harvest if we do not give up."
GALATIANS 6:9, ESV

"Winners never quit, and quitters never win."
-VINCE LOMBARDI

When I think of day "ten" in your journey, I think it is very significant. You are almost halfway through your journey! You will recall that Daniel and his three friends requested the chief official under Nebuchadnezzar to test them for "ten" days by giving them nothing but vegetables to eat and water to drink. Daniel and his three friends did not want to defile themselves with the royal food and wine of the king. This was a partial fast.

What captures my attention is that they did not falter. They did not abandon the fast. I can imagine the "what ifs" that filled their minds. They certainly did not want the chief official of Nebuchadnezzar, in whom they had found favor, to be beheaded. They pressed forward. They did not falter. They had a plan, and they stuck to it. Perhaps Satan, the deceiver, has tempted you to just bow out of the commitment you made and the fast you have chosen.

Don't falter! The word falter means to "walk unsteadily, to stumble, to give way, to move waveringly or hesitantly." Let me encourage you that just as Daniel and his three friends were better nourished than those who ate the royal food, you will be spiritually enriched as you continue to pray, fast, worship, read the Word, and wait on God. They did not see the results of their commitment on the first day, but at the end of the tenth day, it was obvious. You may not see all that God is doing in these ten days as you fast and pray, but you will see how God has worked in your life. Do not falter!

Do not faint! This word signifies a lack of courage and spirit, a lack of strength or vigor, a loss of heart or courage. It can be physical or spiritual. Depending on the type of fast you are doing, you may feel physically tired or hungry, lacking vigor or strength. Or perhaps you are not physically or medically able to fast, but you have been sincerely praying. However, spiritually, your courage and spirit may seem to wane. David encouraged himself in the Lord. The best way to encourage your spirit is to read the Word of God and to continue to pray even if you haven't seen any apparent changes.

In Galatians 6:9, the apostle Paul encourages believers not to grow weary in doing good, for in due season they will reap if they do not faint. You have a season of reaping ahead of you. You have

DAY 10

been sowing spiritual seeds that are going to bear spiritual fruit in the future!

God told Daniel on a different occasion that on the first day of his twenty-one-day fast that He heard his prayer. Daniel received a revelation that he was fighting a spiritual battle. When you pray, or when you pray and fast, you are fighting a spiritual battle, but you are also sowing spiritual seeds. The law of the harvest is that when you sow, you reap. I believe that when you sow into prayer or sow in prayer accompanied with fasting, you will reap a spiritual harvest.

In Luke 18:1, Jesus encouraged his disciples to "pray and not faint." As we fast and pray, we must maintain our strength and resilience to push forward in this spiritual exercise. This verse highlights the importance of maintaining strength and resilience during difficult times. Any lack of perseverance reveals a deficiency in one's inner strength.

Paul encouraged the Thessalonians, "As for you brothers, do not grow weary in doing good" (II Thessalonians 3:13, ESV). The Greek word rendered "grow weary" is *ekkakeo* and appears six times in the New Testament. In secular Greek, it was used to describe a warrior who would shrink from his responsibilities or turn cowardly in the face of conflict. It refers not merely to sore muscles, but to the urge to throw in the towel.[52]

Don't fail! In the film entitled "*The Patriot*," Mel Gibson plays the role of Colonel Benjamin Martin, who, after tragically losing two of his sons during the war, became discouraged and defeated. However, he remembered his deceased wife's words, "Stay the Course." These words became a powerful force in his heart, and he plunged forward with new strength and vigor into the war.

Stay the course! When you fail, your influence weakens. Satan wants to see you fail in completing the 21 days of prayer and fasting, but *Stay the Course!* Persevere because perseverance is an essential element in growing your faith. God desires that you persevere. Trust in God to strengthen you spiritually and physically.

Perhaps the greatest figure in the New Testament who embodies steadfastness, perseverance, and whose desire not to fail was the Apostle Paul. In 2 Corinthians 11:22-28, Paul spoke of the sufferings he endured as a minister of Christ. He spoke of being whipped, stoned, imprisoned, shipwrecked, enduring perils of water, persecution, his own countrymen and Gentiles, perils in the city, wilderness, the sea, and false brethren . Note also he stated that there were times of weariness and toil, sleeplessness, often in hunger and thirst, ***in fastings often*** (emphasis mine), often in cold and nakedness..." We are not told of the number of fastings, what type of fastings he participated, or how often he fasted. Understanding his perseverance and steadfast, one may assume that when he determined to fast for a period that he stayed the course and did not fail in his attempts.

Let me encourage you to continue in this 21-day journey, "Don't falter, faint, or fail." And at the same time, remember this is a time of humbling yourself before God and drawing near to Him.

DAY 11
PRIDE, PRETENSE, OR PASSION

The Pharisee stood and prayed thus with himself: "God, I thank You that I am not like other men—extortioners, unjust, adulterers, or even like this tax collector. I fast twice a week; I give tithes on all that I possess."

LUKE 18: 11-12, ESV

"Humility and knowledge in poor clothes excel pride and ignorance in costly attire."

- WILLIAM PENN

As you begin this day, you are halfway through your 21 days of fasting and prayer. Has God been speaking to you? Has he challenged your heart? Solomon wrote, "Above all else, guard your heart, for everything you do flows from it" (Proverbs 4:23, NIV). Keep pressing forward with all your heart!

"The heart is deceitful above all things and desperately wicked; who can know it" (Jeremiah 17:9, NKJV)? Jeremiah was describing the sinful nature of every human being, the heart being the center of our personality or the totality of our inner being. Jesus said, "For from within, out of the heart of man, come evil thoughts, sexual immorality, theft, murder, adultery, coveting, wickedness, deceit, sensuality, envy, slander, pride, foolishness," (Mark 7:21, ESV).

Jesus told a parable about two men, a Pharisee and a tax collector, who went to the temple to pray. The Pharisee, full of himself, declared his proposed righteousness, contrasting himself with the tax collector. In his deceitful pride, he commented that he fasted twice a week and was a man who tithed on all that he possessed.

Did you notice he was proud of fasting? Pride can be subtle. As Christians, we must guard our hearts. Like this Pharisee, we can be proud of our fasting and even compare ourselves with others who are not fasting. Satan fell because of his pride. We need not replicate his action.

We must search our hearts and examine our motivation for fasting. A person who candidly boasts about how long they have fasted or when they fast seeks the accolades of men. A person may impose upon themselves a false sense of superiority while looking down upon another person with disdain. The appearance of superiority makes a very ludicrous figure. Jesus called such a Pharisee a hypocrite, one who was wearing a mask and playing a part. He was being what he was not.

Fasting is not a discipline meant to attract the attention of others. It is a spiritual practice in which we set aside our pride and humble ourselves before God. The goal is not to be seen. Most fasting should be done in secret before our Heavenly Father, who will graciously re-

DAY 11

ward us. This does not imply that corporate fasting is wrong. When you pray and fast with others corporately, your fasting becomes known, but the motivation is to humbly unite in seeking the face of God. This can be a powerful experience for a group of believers. If this is not the goal, such corporate fasting is pretentious, fraudulent, and will be a failed exercise.

Fasting can be a means of developing a love for God, a passion for God. When we fast silently throughout the day, it may be the expression of the inarticulate cry of the soul. Your stomach is craving physical food, but your soul is craving and crying out for more of God. David's passionate longing for God is colorfully expressed, "O God, you are my God; earnestly I seek you; my soul thirsts for you..." (Psalm 63:1, ESV). "As the deer pants for flowing streams, so pants my soul for you, O God" (Psalm 42:1, ESV).

I believe that fasting can express a hunger in our souls for more of God. Though we can earn nothing from God through our fasting, fasting shows a resolved determination, a sincere desire, a laser-like focus, and an alignment of our hearts to hunger and thirst passionately after God and to experience His presence.

A. W. Tozer succinctly summed up the purpose of his book, *The Fire of God's Presence*, stating, "The presence of God is not something we talk about. It is rather something we experience."[53] Engaging in fasting and prayer during these twenty-one days will contribute immensely to experiencing His life-changing presence.

DAY 12: FASTING FOR A SPIRITUAL BREAKTHROUGH

"Do not fear, Daniel, for from the first day that you set your heart to understand, to humble yourself before God, your words were heard: and I have come because of your word."

DANIEL 10:12, KJV

"Fasting can bring breakthroughs in the spiritual realm that will never happen in any other way."

-RICHARD FOSTER

Have you entered a season of 21 days of prayer and fasting looking for a spiritual breakthrough in your life? If so, I believe with all my heart that sincere fasting and praying can give you your desired spiritual breakthrough. What exactly is a "spiritual breakthrough?" The context limits it to an event that occurs in our spiritual life. It is a significant, sudden, stupendous, and often supernatural and providential intervention in one's spiritual battle that results in overcoming an object, deliverance from bondage, bringing transformation, freedom, and victory.

Jim Cymbala, in his book *Breakthrough Prayer,* wrote, "We desperately need a spiritual breakthrough so we can experience triumphant joy rather than the gloom and lifelessness we often see in our churches."[54] Jesus knew of breakthrough joy. He declared, "Hitherto have you asked nothing in my name: ask, and ye shall receive, that your joy may be full (John 16:24, KJV).

Richard Foster, in his book entitled *Celebration of Discipline,* wrote, "Fasting can bring breakthroughs in the spiritual realm that will never happen in any other way. It is a means of God's grace and blessing that should not be neglected any longer."[55]

Fasting, as we have seen, is a spiritual discipline and is effective in helping us to pray when many times we do not feel like praying. When Christ faced his greatest challenge of going to the cross of Calvary, he asked his disciples to pray. They could not pray for one hour before giving in to the weakness of their flesh. Jesus pointed out the weakness of our flesh when he stated, "The spirit is willing, but the flesh is weak" (Matthew 26:41, ESV). If we utilize the discipline of fasting, we may quickly discover more power to pray. "The tandem of prayer and fasting will give you the power and willpower to pray through until you experience a breakthrough."[56]

Perhaps you entered 21 days of fasting and prayer looking for a physical miracle. You need the supernatural physical healing of your body. You are in an impossible situation. Well, you have a God who can make the impossible possible. Why not seek God with fasting and prayer?

Andrew Murray wrote, "Fasting helps to express, to deepen, and to confirm the resolution that we are ready to sacrifice anything, even ourselves, to attain the kingdom of God."[57]

DAY 12

Elmer Towns stated that the students at Liberty University fasted for spiritual breakthroughs and commented that in 1985, 5,000 students prayed for the physical healing of their Dean of Students, Veron Brewer. Vernon had cancer. God healed Vernon, and over 30 years later, he is involved in foreign missions.[58]

We need to be reminded that fasting is not an entitlement. We merit nothing. Fasting complements prayer. Fasting humbles our hearts and souls before God. It demonstrates our sincere recognition of our deep need for His grace, mercy, and love in our lives, while acknowledging His divine sovereignty.

God answers prayer based on His goodness, not ours. When He sovereignly heals or chooses not to heal, He does so because of who He is. And He is infinitely good, kind, merciful, just, wise, and loving. We never pray amiss when we humble our hearts in fasting and bring our petitions to Him.

A great biblical illustration of this is a woman named Hannah. You may recall that she lived with her husband (Elkanah), but she shared her husband with another woman who was also the wife of Elkanah. Her name was Peninnah. Peninnah was fertile, and Hannah was infertile, and Peninnah constantly provoked and tormented her. This went on for years, and one day, after years of grief and agitation, Hannah prayed a prayer that changed not only her destiny but also the destiny of the nation of Israel.

As she traveled to Shiloah, the Bible said Hannah wept and would not eat (perhaps some intermittent fasting taking place). When she reached the temple, she prayed. In her prayer, she stated that if God would give her a son; she would give him back (dedicate him) to the

Lord by giving him to Eli the priest, thus giving him to the Lord's work. Her prayer was one of great intensity and sincerity.

She needed a physical breakthrough! We may assume that it was very emotional. She poured her entire being into this prayer—body, soul, and spirit—and her silent tears spoke volumes. God heard her soft prayers, in which only her lips moved. It was not her words that God heard; it was her heart, the center of her personality, crying out to God. She did what some saints refer to as *praying through,* and somehow deep within her, she knew God had answered her prayer. The impossible was made possible, despair was turned into joy, and praise to the Lord flowed effortlessly from her spirit, soul, and mouth. She was pregnant!

Hannah was not only a woman of prayer; she was a woman of integrity. "She vowed a vow and said, 'Lord of hosts, if you will indeed look on the affliction of your servant and remember me and not forget your servant, but will give to your servant a son, then I will give him to the Lord all the days of his life, and no razor shall touch his head'" (1 Samuel 1:11, ESV). She kept her vow and after Samuel, who was around three years old, was weaned; she presented him to Eli the priest, thus dedicating him to the Lord.

Her sacrifice and integrity did not go unnoticed by the Lord. The Bible declares, "Indeed the Lord visited Hannah, and she conceived and bore three sons and two daughters. And the boy Samuel grew in the presence of the Lord" (1 Samuel 2:21, ESV). I wonder how great an impact a mother like Hannah, a woman of faith, who prayed and fasted, had on these five children? We read in the scriptures that Elkanah's other wife, Peninnah, had two sons, Hophni and Phine-

DAY 12

has. They were having sex with the women who were serving at the entrance to the tent of meeting, and God's judgment would fall on them, both dying on the same day. But we read nothing negative regarding Hannah's other five children.

Friend, do you need a physical breakthrough, a supernatural work of God in your body? God has not changed. He resists the proud but gives grace to the humble. Humble your soul with fasting, seek Him earnestly, pray without ceasing, and believe He is able. As you fast and pray, you can become a candidate for the sovereign working power of an all-powerful God.

People often pray more earnestly in times of serious need. We acknowledge the seriousness of the need and are fully aware that we desperately need God in His divine providence to intervene on our behalf. We follow a logical path, recognizing our needs and God's provision. We almost effortlessly quote scriptures that speak of His promises of provision.

For example, we may quote the scripture, "My God shall supply all my needs according to his riches in Christ Jesus." (Philippians 4:13) However, in quoting the scripture of provision, we have moved from simply declaring a promise to the stark reality that we must have God's intervening help. This is the mindset of a "breakthrough" prayer. It is a prayer that is based on the seriousness of our need, and the character of God, not just his promises. It is Esther fasting and praying, three days without food or water, to a "covenant-keeping God" for the deliverance of her people. And God powerfully and providentially breaks through!

Perhaps you are in the valley of decision, and you need a word from God, or as one dear saint prayed, "She needed a word from the Word." Oftentimes, God speaks at just the right time, a word from the Word. That word provides guidance and direction. For example, while seeking guidance, a scripture captures your mind. Aye, a word from the Word! It may be Proverbs 3:5-6, "Trust in the Lord with all your heart and lean not to your own understanding, in all your ways acknowledge him, and he shall direct thy paths." As you silently resign to simply trust God, circumstances, people, or simple solutions will appear in your life at just the right moment. It's a breakthrough moment.

Or perhaps, it is a prophetic word that comes your way at just the right time, or a providential circumstance has unfolded. It is a spiritual breakthrough. However, we must be careful; positive circumstances do not necessarily indicate that one is in the will of God. Jonah found a ship going to Joppa, but God wanted him to go to Nineveh. And negative circumstances are not necessarily a sign that you are out of God's will. Paul was headed to Rome when a fierce storm interrupted his plans, and he found himself, along with others, stranded on an island (Malta). But the interruption was God's plan!

Jim Cymbal wrote, "The Spirit is still alive and active on the earth. No passage in the Bible teaches us to no longer expect the Holy Spirit's word of guidance in whatever manner he might bring it. The Spirit still desires to guide, but he needs people with an ear to hear what he's saying."[59]

DAY 13
FASTING AND YOUR BODY

"Do you not know that your bodies are the temple of the Holy Spirit, who is in you, whom you have received from God? You are not your own;"
1 CORINTHIANS 6:19, NIV

"Fasting of the body is food for the soul."
-SAINT JOHN CHRYSOSTOM

As Christians, we rejoice that Jesus Christ has redeemed our souls. Paul eloquently stated, "In him we have redemption through his blood, the forgiveness of sins, in accordance with the riches of God's grace that he lavished upon us" (Ephesians 1:7-8, NIV).

The body is now the temple of the Holy Spirit. But our bodies are not yet redeemed. Our bodies will one day die. Paul declared, "And not only that, but also we ourselves, having the first fruits of the Spirit, even we groan within ourselves, waiting eagerly for our adoption as sons and daughters, the redemption of our bodies" (Romans 8:23, KJV). Until we receive our glorified body, we have this earthly body, and we should take good care of our bodies because they are the temple of the Holy Spirit, who dwells in us.

The Vanderbilt University School of Medicine conducted a study of the breaking of carbohydrates, fats, and proteins during a fast. Mary Ruth Swope in her book *The Roots & Fruits of Fasting* wrote of their findings. "The findings, printed in the American Journal of Clinical Nutrition (60:29-36) showed that during a fast, the body shifts its energy source from starches and sugary foods (carbohydrates) to fat."[60]

Fasting and prayer can help you conquer your appetite and learn to say no to your flesh. Not only will you become spiritually healthier, but you will become physically healthy. When you fast, you allow your body to rid itself of harmful toxins in your blood, liver, skin, and lungs. Individuals can also enjoy lowering their blood pressure, cholesterol, and fatty acids during these twenty-one days. Another aspect of fasting is the physiological change in the white blood cells of our body. When we fast, white blood cells become "better equipped to destroy harmful bacteria."[61]

I remember when I was a young boy, after a long winter in West Virginia, my mother would do what she called *spring cleaning*. During the winter, dirt and dust would be tracked into different areas of the house. When beautiful spring days arrived, she deep-cleaned the house and opened the windows, and the refreshing smell of spring air would fill the room. Fasting is a lot like spring cleaning. It is a designated time for the body to be refreshed and our souls to be rejuvenated by God.

DAY 13

People usually eat three meals a day and some snacks in between. When we fast, we give the organs of our body rest. This would be the stomach, intestines, pancreas, and gallbladder. In addition, the liver has an opportunity to rest from the filtering process of the blood and to detoxify. We hear a lot about how hard our heart works. However, Dr. Don Cobert, in his book *Fasting Zone,* stated, "The hardest-working organ in the body is the liver. Weighing about three pounds, it is also the largest organ inside the body, about the size of a football."[62]

Fasting promotes blood sugar control by reducing insulin resistance... promotes better health by fighting inflammation... May enhance heart health by improving blood pressure, triglycerides, and cholesterol levels...May boost brain function and prevent neurodegenerative...May aid weight loss by limitation of calories and boosting. metabolism... May increase growth hormone secretions...Could extend longevity...May aid in cancer prevention. [63]

In his book, *Fasting for Spiritual Breakthrough,* Elmer L. Towns included an appendix written by Dr. Rex Russel (a medical doctor) who wrote that Dr. George Thampy, a biochemist at the University of Indiana wrote of a research done on sixty healthy people who fasted 21days in which the results show of significant lowering of their cholesterol, lowering of their blood pressure, relief from arthritis, and loss of 40 pounds.[64]

We are living in the age of stress and anxiety. Though stress is a natural reaction to external situations or circumstances, over a prolonged period; it can contribute to mental health and physical conditions. It is reported that "nearly 90 percent of adults in the United States" lose sleep because of anxiety or worry about their health or the economy."[65] The 2024 results of the American Psychiatric Association's annual mental health poll show that U.S. adults are feeling anxious and in 2024, 43% of adults say they feel more anxious than they did the previous year.[66]

Arthur Wallis wrote, "In an age of pressure, when the breakdown of mind and body among professing Christians is becoming all too familiar, the physical value of a fast of God choosing becomes a matter of some importance."[67] Fasting for 21 days may very well be a time for the renewal not just for our spirit and soul but also for our mind and body.

Franklin Jentezen pointed out significant benefits from fasting. "Fastens sharpen your mental process and aids and improves your sight, hearing, taste, touch, smell, and all sensory faculties.[68]

Mary Ruth Swoope who received a Master of Science degree in foods and nutrition from the Women's College of the University of North Carolina— Greensboro College, in her book entitled, *The Roots & Fruits of Fasting* wrote that she "Discovered research supporting the idea that fasting helps relieve the symptoms of, or even completely heal, a variety of different diseases and medical conditions." [69] She stated that "Fasting can heal people of allergies, asthma, bladder disease, bursitis, hay fever, high blood pressure, kidney disease, nervous exhaustion, obesity, poor circulation, rheumatism, schizophrenia, skin disease, and stress. [70] She did not, however, reference any resources documenting such cures.

DAY 13

Isaiah the prophet's words on fasting should ring a bell as we note the physical and spiritual benefits of fasting. "Then shall your light break forth like the dawn, and your healing shall spring up speedily; Your righteousness shall go before you; The glory of the Lord shall be your rear guard" (Isaiah 58:8, ESV).

 # FASTING AND PRAYER

"...She never left the temple but worshipped night and day, fasting and praying."
LUKE 2:37, NIV

"Prayer needs fasting for its full growth. Prayer is the one hand with which we grasp the invisible. Fasting is the other hand, the one with which we let go of the visible."
-ANDREW MURRAY

If you have been a part of corporate prayer, or if you have individually selected to fast and pray for 21 days, then you are about to complete two weeks and will be two-thirds through the fast. Throughout this book, you have noticed how fasting and prayer are joined together. We pointed out that if you are fasting without praying; you are dieting. And if you are fasting without positioning your heart for prayer, you are simply experiencing hunger without experiencing God.

Every kind of magnet has two poles, and even if you cut a magnet in half, each half will automatically have two poles. The interesting facts are that the opposite poles of a magnet attract, and the same poles of a magnet repel. Fasting and prayer are like two opposite poles of a magnet that naturally go together. Visualize fasting as the north pole and prayer as the south pole. Even though much emphasis has been placed on fasting, we are not ignoring the necessity and great importance of prayer.

The great importance of prayer is magnified when we consider our redemption that we have in Christ Jesus. The writer of the book of Hebrews wrote, "Neither by the blood of goats and calves but by his own blood he entered in once into the holy place having obtain eternal redemption for us" (Hebrews 9:12, KJV). It is because of the blood of Jesus that we have access into the very presence of God. The writer emphatically stated, "Having therefore, brethren, boldness to enter into the Holiest by the blood of Jesus" (Hebrews 10:19, KJV). The great expositor, David Martin Llyod Jones wrote of this verse that, "There is no more important text in the Bible, I sometimes think than that."[71] He further stated, "That is the whole secret of prayer, and we do not know what prayer is unless we really grasp the meaning of that great statement."[72]

The Gospel of Matthew 7:7-8 contains two powerful scripture verses on prayer. Jesus said, "Ask and it will be given unto you; seek and you will find; knock and the door will be opened to you. For everyone who asks receives; he who seeks finds; and to him who knocks the door will be opened" (Mattthew 7:7-8, NIV).

DAY 14

Let us first look at the words "ask, seek, and knock." There are certainly both a progression and an intensity. The first step is to petition God. But it is more than petitioning. There is the element of being laser-focused. There is something specific that you are praying for. There is no ambiguity or pious wishing. There is a definite petition to meet a definite need. For example, it may be a serious financial need. A prayer may be vocalized as such, "Father, I need one thousand dollars to purchase a used car so that I can travel back and forth to work. Father, would you in your goodness meet this need?"

God knows the need even before we pray. We, however, need to ask because it enables us to communicate with our Heavenly Father. Our prayer is based upon a filial relationship we have with God. Our asking expresses our sincere faith and builds a loving and deep relationship with Him. It is an opportunity for us to (humbly) acknowledge our dependence on Him and to seek His divine guidance and provision, and to experience His goodness.

The Greek tense here (present active indicative) would render the text, "Keep on asking."

The request is a definite request for a need, for a definite period (as long as it takes). Jesus does not want us to give up on asking.

The second step is to seek God. When we seek God, we are diligently continuing to approach our Heavenly Father in prayer, earnestly and with great anticipation for the answer to our petition. There is a sense of expectation. The Greek tense is the same, and thus rendered, "Keep on seeking." Once again, there is no pious wishing or ambiguity. Continuing to seek God is more than just having our requests answered. In this process of seeking, we are developing a personal relationship with a personal God. We are cultivating an awareness of His presence and drawing near to Him, and while concerned with our needs, we are focused on Him. Jeremiah wrote, "The LORD is good to those who wait for Him, To the person who seeks Him" (Lamentations 3:24, NASV).

The third step in praying is to "knock." Knocking emphasizes an "insistence, persistence." Once again, the Greek tense equates to "Keep on Knocking." It goes beyond casual praying or passively waiting for God to answer your prayer. It is a "spiritual knocking" that refuses to take a seeming "no" as an answer. It is a determination that refuses to be discouraged because of a delay in an immediate response. There is a continual, deliberate and perhaps forceful action with high expectation of a response. It is a persevering faith in action. Jesus told a story that paints a picture of the need, and the intensity or energy expended in obtaining the need.

> Suppose one of you have a friend, and he goes to him at midnight and says, 'Friend, lend me three loaves of bread, because a friend of mine on a journey has come to me, and I have nothing to set before him.' Then the one inside answers, 'Don't bother me. The door is already locked, and my children are with me in bed. I can't get up and give you anything.' I tell you, though he will not get up and give him the bread because he is his fried, yet because of the man's boldness he will get up and give him as much as he needs.[73]

The following verse explains why we should continually ask, seek, and knock. "For everyone who asks receives; he who seeks finds; and

DAY 14

to him who knocks the door will be opened" (Matthew 7:8, NIV). In the Greek language, the word "for" is *gar*. It's a conjunction or particle. The translation would be "because" or "since." Gar introduces to the reader the reason or the explanation of the clause tied to the preceding scripture (Ask, and it will be given to you; seek and seek and you will find; knock and the door will be opened to you). This is powerful!

The child of God asks, seeks, and knocks because God has promised to answer the petition. We know that "God is not a man, that he should lie, nor a son of man, that he should change his mind" (Numbers 23:19, NIV).

Here are a few other references in which we see the use of the conjunction *gar* in the book of Matthew and Hebrews.

- Matthew 1:21 (KJV)- "And ye shall bring forth a son, and thou shalt call his name Jesus for (*gar*) he shall save his people from their sins." The name Jesus means "Savior, or God saves."
- Matthew 2:5 (KJV)- "And they said unto him, In Bethlehem of Judea: (*gar*) thus it is written by the prophet." The reason the chief priests and scribes informed Herod that Christ was born in Bethlehem for (*gar*), because Bethlehem was prophesied as the place. Note the prophecy, "And thou Bethlehem, in the land of Judah are not the least among the princes in Juda for (*gar*) out of thee shall come a Governor, that shall rule my people Israel" (Matthew 2:6, KJV).
- Matthew 4:18 (KJV)- "And Jesus, walking by the sea of Galilee, saw two brethren, Simon called Peter, and Andrew his

brother, casting a net into the sea; for (gar) they were fishers." The reason Simon and Peter were casting a net into the sea is because they were fishermen.

- Hebrews 11:6 (NIV) "And without faith it is impossible to please God, because (*gar*) anyone who comes to him must believe that he exists and that he rewards those who earnestly seek him."

In each of the above examples, you see the word *gar* (for or because) functioning as a conjunction introducing a reason, explanation, or justification for a preceding statement. When you see the word "for" or "because," ask yourself, "What is *gar* explaining?" Note how we consider the context of the scripture and gain a greater comprehension of the scripture.

During these 21 days of fasting and prayer, let's not grow weary, let's not give up but diligently pray. God's unchanging character is the foundation for the promise of answered prayer.

DAY 15
THE WARFARE OF FASTING AND PRAYER

"For we do not wrestle against flesh and blood, but against the rulers, against the authorities, against the cosmic powers over this present darkness, against spiritual forces of evil in the heavenly places."

EPHESIANS 6:12, ESV

"When God opens the windows of heaven to bless us, the devil will open the doors of hell to blast us."

—AUTHOR UNKNOWN[74]

Ephesians 6:12 categorically states that the saints of God are living in a world in which there are spiritual adversaries and that there are times in which we are engaged in warfare against such opponents. Not that we are looking for a demon in every corner, but we can with certainty expect to encounter spiritual resistance. Satan will seek to hinder you from praying and fasting. Satan may endeavor to tempt and oppress a warring saint, but we need not be discouraged, defeated. We can triumphantly quote the Apostle John's words, "They overcame him (Satan) because of the blood of the Lamb and because of the word of their testimony… (Revelation 12:11, KJV)

Jesus was able to resist the temptations of the devil as he fasted and prayed. It is interesting to note that our Savior did not enter public ministry of healing the sick or casting out demons until after he had fasted and prayed for forty days.

No doubt, the chief adversary is Satan. The word "adversary" means accuser, coming from the root word to oppose. He has many different names in the Bible. The Bible references him as Lucifer, which means "morning star," implying the brightness of his character or beauty before his fall from heaven. He is called Beelzebub, prince of the demons, Abaddon which means "destruction," Apollyon, Greek for "destroyer," Belial meaning "worthless," The Devil, Serpent (representing temptation), The Tempter, (tempting men towards disobedience), The Adversary, (an opponent) Accuser, (accusing us before God), The Evil One, (his pernicious character) The Prince and power of the air, (rank of authority in wicked spiritual realm), and Father of lies, (his deceitful nature).

Satan has under him various ranks of diabolical spirits. Daniel was a student of the Word of God and understood that Jeremiah the prophet had promised seventy years of captivity for the nation of Israel. He sought God for the fulfillment of promises, putting on sackcloth, ashes, and fasting.

God revealed to Daniel during a 21-day fast for the people of Israel that a spiritual adversary named the Prince of Persia was responsible for the delay of Daniel's prayer. The angel informed Daniel that

DAY 15

his prayer had been heard on the very first day of prayer and fasting. Daniel received insight into the wicked prince of Persia and another prince named the prince of Greece. There are different ranks of evil spirits under the rule of Satan.

As a person reads of Daniel's 21-day fast, it is undeniable that Daniel's fast was instrumental in breaking the power of Satan's nefarious spirits and the dispatching of angelic beings to accomplish God's sovereign purposes.

The *Baker Encyclopedia of Psychology & Counseling* states that, "The New Testament includes more than one hundred references to the existence of demons." (H.A. Virkler)[75] Jesus candidly taught the reality of demons and their ability to cause different physical and mental disorders. His ministry included the expulsion of demons.

Satan not only has different names, commands different levels of nefarious spirits, but he also has different schemes. When you are successful in overcoming one of his nefarious plans, he will often use a different plan. Paul wrote that we as Christians are not ignorant of his "schemes", (2 Corinthians 2:11, NASB).

The Greek word for schemes is *noema,* which means thoughts. Dr. A. T. Robertson wrote that "*noema* is derived from *noeo,* to use the *nous* is an old word, especially for evil plans and purposes here."[76] This word incorporates the idea not just of schemes but also of plans, plots, and purposes of Satan.

Satan has been around a long time and has had a long time to hone his skills. When you are engaged in spiritual warfare with fasting and prayer, the Holy Spirit can give you insight into Satan's various devices.

On the natural level, we don't have spiritual insight into Satan's activities, but God does, and Paul stated we are not ignorant of his schemes.

People often say, "It is what it is." Even God's people frequently echo this phrase. Things are not always what they are. The child of God can have a heart capable of knowing when things could be the nefarious works of the enemy. Charles Spurgeon stated, "Discernment sees through the enemy's schemes."[77] Paul wrote to the Thessalonians, "For we wanted to come to you—I, Paul, more than once—and Satan hindered us" (I Thessalonians 2:18, NASB). The word "hindered" is the Greek word *enkopto* which means "to cut in, to hinder." The verb, used to cut in a road, "was to make a road impassable."[78] God can reveal the schemes, the plotting, the planning, the thoughts, and the maneuvering of Satan. Satan seeks to hinder our paths and the work God wants to do through us, especially when it comes to spiritual warfare.

The Christian engaged in spiritual warfare need not be afraid and need not think that the enemy will triumph. When Jesus sent out his twelve disciples, he said, "And as ye go, preach, saying the kingdom of heaven is at hand. Heal the sick, raise the dead, cleanse the lepers, cast demons. Freely ye have received, freely give" (Matthew 10:8 7-8, NASB). That is a powerful mandate!

The Apostle Paul declared, in Romans 8:37 (NASB), "But in all these things (tribulation, distress, persecution, famine, nakedness, peril or sword mentioned in Romans 8:35) we 'overwhelmingly conquer' through Him who loved us." Paul was further convinced, "That neither death, nor life, nor angels, nor principalities, nor things pres-

DAY 15

ent nor things to come, nor powers, nor height, nor depth, nor any other created thing will be able to separate us form the love of God, which is in Christ Jesus" (Romans 8:38-39, NASB).

Paul prayed for the Ephesian believers that they would be enlightened, know the hope of God's calling, the riches of the glory of his inheritance in the saints, and the surpassing greatness of his divine power. He pointed out that such divine power is the same divine power that raised Christ from the dead. Note how Phillip paraphrased the divine power of God in Ephesians 1:19-20.

That power is the same divine power that was demonstrated in Christ when He raised Him from the dead and gave him the place of supreme honor in Heaven—a place that is, infinitely superior to any perceivable command, authority, power, or control, and which carries with it a name, far beyond any name that could ever be used in this world or the world to come.[79]

Jentezen Franklin wrote, "I have seen people who have never fasted before experience marvelous breakthroughs in their lives."[80] I fully believe that as you continue in these 21 days of fasting, you can expect to see the awesome supernatural power of God intervening in your life.

And not only you, but your family. Some families have struggled for years with some form of demonic attack. Perhaps some of you who are fasting may have come from dysfunctional families where generational curses have followed.

For example, perhaps your mother and father, grandmother and grandfather, and great-grandparents have been bound by alcohol.

There certainly is a higher chance of succeeding generations being alcoholics. Two outstanding generational sins would be sins of witchcraft and the occult that seem to have a tenacious grip. Other sins may be the sins of pride, rebellion, and idolatry. In third-world countries, a generational sin would be ancestor worship. I believe that such generational curses can be broken. I believe as you fast, pray, and commit yourself to the Lordship of Jesus Christ that you and your family are starting a new generational line of believers who will impact the world for Jesus. Your breakthrough may be during your fast or even after your fast. God is a rewarder of those who diligently seek him!

DAY 16: FASTING FOR DECISION MAKING

"So when they had appointed elders in every church and prayed with fasting, they commended them to the Lord in whom they believed."
ACTS 14:23, NKJV

"We fast to seek and submit to God's will."
-DAVID PLATT

It was during a time of fasting that God said, "Set apart for me Barnabas and Saul for the work that I have called them" (Acts 13:2, NASB). Following that prophetic word, some members of the church at Antioch fasted and prayed and laid their hands upon Saul and Barnabas and sent them on the First Missionary Journey. Was this a major decision? Yes!

Paul and Barnabus had returned to Lystra, Iconium, and Antioch. Luke writes, "When they had appointed elders in every church, having prayed with fasting, they commended them to the Lord in whom they had believed" (Acts 14:23, NASB). Choosing spiritual leaders was not something Paul and Barnabas did lightly. They sought guidance from God as they prayed and fasted before making a choice.

It is interesting to note that when Jesus was to decide as to whom he would call to be disciples that Jesus went off to the mountain to pray, and He spent the whole night in prayer to God and in the morning, "He called His disciples to Him and chose twelve of them whom he also name as apostles" (Luke 6:12-13, NASB).

It was on a Sabbath day that Jesus healed a man with a withered hand. Some of the Pharisees were enraged that the Lord had healed on the Sabbath and were discussing among themselves "what they may do to Jesus" (Luke 6:11, NASB). Matthew wrote that "It was at this time" that Jesus had gone to the mountain to pray.

We do not know what time of the day Jesus left or when he reached the mountain. Did He take food with Him? We are not told. Did He take water with Him? We are not told. Did He fast during those critical hours? We are not told. However, it may be assumed that while He prayed all night long that He could have fasted. Was it a major decision? Yes! The spreading of good news, the gospel, would be contingent upon whom He trained and the outpouring of the Holy Spirit.

John tells the story of Jesus feeling a divine compulsion to go through Samaria. It was a major spiritual decision. "He had to pass through Samaria" (John 4:4, NASB). Why? There was a Samaritan woman who would embrace him as the Messiah, and because of her experience, many Samaritans would believe in Christ as the Savior of the world (John 4:39, 42, NASB). That's awesome! But let's look at the whole story.

DAY 16

Jesus was in Sychar, a city in Samaria. His disciples had gone into the city to purchase some food. At Jacob's well, Jesus, weary and hungry from the journey from Judea, sat down at this well and began a dialogue with a woman. He would ask her to draw him a drink from the well, while all the time, he was drawing her to Him. When the disciples came back, they saw Jesus speaking with the Samaritan woman. They questioned him and soon discovered His mission.

It is interesting to note that Jesus had fasted for the time the disciples left until they returned with food. His disciples urged him to eat. He refused and said, "I have food to eat that you do not know about" (John 4:32, NASB). This caused some uncertainty. Who had provided him with food? They said to one another, "No one brought Him anything to eat, did he" (John 4:33, NASB)?

Jesus had been on a mission! It certainly was an important mission. He must have been just as hungry as the disciples who scurried off for food. But the food that he talked about was the enrichment of his life by fulfilling the Father's will by touching a broken life.

What major spiritual decisions do you have to make to do the Father's will? What will it cost you? Would it be a meal or something greater than a meal? What impact will your decision have on the kingdom of God? The spiritual discipline of prayer and fasting may be very instrumental in helping you to make whatever decision you must make. Perhaps it is a job, a marriage, a financial investment, moving, stepping out in faith on a missionary journey, hiring an employee, adopting a baby, or spiritually hungering for more of God. There can be a plethora of things to do. It would be wise to slow down and pray about it. Depending on how serious the decision is that we are making, we may resort to prayer and fasting.

Fasting and prayer may follow a decision you have already made. Sometimes we can make wrong decisions. Joshua is a classical illustration. "So the men of Israel took some of their provisions, and did not ask for the counsel of the Lord" (Joshua 9:14, NASB). Israel had entered the Promised Land, and they were wiping out their enemies, defeating some at Jericho and at Ai. The Gibeonites heard about Joshua's victories and crafted a scheme to deceive Joshua. "Joshua made peace with them and made a covenant with them, to let them live; and the leaders of the congregation swore an oath unto them" (Joshua 9:15, NASB). Our wrong decisions may push us into serious prayer and fasting, asking God for his divine intervention and assistance.

DAY 17: THE NECESSITY OF WAITING ON GOD

"And therefore will the Lord wait, that he may be gracious unto you, and therefore will he be exalted, that he may have mercy upon you: for the Lord is a God of judgment: blessed are all they that wait for him."
ISAIAH 30:18, KJV

"God waits for you and me to wait for Him."
- WALTER H. BEUTTLER

As you seek the Lord during this season of prayer and fasting, you must devote time to waiting on God. Prayer is not a monologue. It is a dialogue. When you spend time silently waiting on God, you provide an opportunity for God to talk to you. There are times in our spiritual life when we often reach a spiritual plateau. When you silently wait on God, you allow God to take you to a new height. "… That He may be gracious to you."

David wrote, "Be still, and know that I am God…" (Psalm 46:10, NKJV)! The New American Standard Bible translates, "Cease striving and know that I am God..." As we sit still in His presence and wait on God, we intentionally create space for Him. In the book entitled *Waiting on the Lord,* Walter H. Beuttler wrote, "The very grandeur and omnipotence and greatness of God silences the human spirit. Be still, be silent."[81] This act of worshipful silence is a time when you can incorporate admiration, adoration, and inner praise as your spirit quietly reaches up to God.

Isaiah wrote, "For since the beginning of the world men have not heard, nor perceived by the ear, neither hath the eye seen, O God beside thee, what he hath prepared for him that waiteth for him" (Isaiah 64:4, KJV). In Hebrew, the phrase, "what he hath prepared for him that waiteth for him," is, "Who worketh for him that hath waited for him." When we quietly wait in His presence, God begins to set something in motion. "He worketh for him that waited for him."

Let's wait in his presence and discover what he has been waiting to do in us and for us.

When you wait on God, there may be times when you feel nothing. It is during these times that "naked faith" believes God is working when we can't see Him working. We simply need to "Wait patiently for the Lord; be strong and take heart and wait for the Lord" (Psalm 27:14, NLT). David wrote, "I waited patiently for the Lord; and he inclined unto me, and heard my cry" (Psalm 40:1, KJV).

Our waiting is never in vain because He whom we wait for is ever present and in due time will come to us. Our waiting is never in vain because He whom we wait for never sleeps or slumbers. Our waiting is never in vain because He whom we wait for is infinitely holy and

DAY 17

without flaw. His character is unimpeachable, and His ear is always inclined toward us.

Paul wrote, "But as it is written, Eye hath not seen, nor ear heard, neither have entered into the heart of man, the things which God hath prepared for them that love him. But God hath revealed them unto us by his Spirit; for the Spirit searcheth all things, yea, the deep things of God" (1 Corinthians 2:9-10, KJV). Walter H. Beuttler felt that "Waiting for God is a precondition for God taking us in the depths of the knowledge of God and the knowledge of His Spirit." [82] Waiting on God is a precondition for receiving illumination or revelation of biblical truth.

Jeremiah wrote, "The Lord is good to those who wait for Him, To the person who seeks him" (Lamentations 3:25, NASB). I believe that the spiritual discipline of waiting on God is indispensable as we seek the face of God with prayer and fasting. God's goodness is infinite, and he longs to demonstrate His goodness in your life. Let's take sufficient time to wait in His presence, to experience God, and revel in His goodness.

David wrote," Wait for the Lord; Be strong and let your heart take courage; Yes, wait for the Lord" (Psalm 27:14, NASB). The Hebrew word for wait is *qavah,* "which means to bind together by twisting, to be bound together with the object of our waiting, and to wait with expectation and hope."[83] Our heart, soul, and spirit are bound together with our God as we wait expectantly in His presence in our pursuit of Him. How awesome it is to wait in His presence for His manifest presence!

As we wait patiently in his presence, we allow God to reveal himself to us. Isaiah the prophet wrote, "And it will be said in that day: 'Behold this is our God; We have waited for Him and He will save us. This is the Lord; We have waited for Him; We will rejoice in His salvation'" (Isaiah 25:9, NKJV). Note that when the church corporately gathers, it is a good thing for us to have time to be quiet and wait together in his presence. It is a time in which we make room for God to reveal Himself to us and to illuminate the Word of God to our hearts.

Have you ever experienced a decline in your spiritual or physical strength? Then listen to the words of Isaiah, who wrote, "Those who wait for the Lord will gain new strength; They will mount up with wings like eagles, They will run and not get tired, They will walk and not become weary" (Isaiah 40:31 (NASB).

Rev. Andrew Murray, who was an advocate for waiting on God, wrote, "Would God that we might get some right conception of what the influence would be on a life spent, not in thought, or imagination or effort, but in the power of the Holy Spirit, wholly waiting upon God."[84]

DAY 18
SIGNS, WONDERS, MIRACLES, AND GIFTS OF THE HOLY SPIRIT

"This salvation, which was first announced by the Lord, was confirmed to those who heard him. God also testified to it by signs, wonders and various miracles, and gifts of the Holy Spirit distributed according to his will."

HEBREWS 2:4, NIV

"Then Jesus (after 40 days of fasting) returned in the power of the Spirit to Galilee..."

LUKE 4:14, NKJV

"Trying to do the Lord's work in your own strength is the most confusing, exhausting, and tedious work. But when you are filled with the Holy Spirit then the ministry of Jesus flows out of you."[85]

-CORRIE TEN BOOM

The New Testament introduces you to a supernatural God doing supernatural things through the lives of ordinary men. Signs, wonders, miracles, and gifts distributed to men by the ever-present Holy Spirit corroborate the gospel message concerning the birth, life, death, resurrection, and ascension of Jesus Christ. Men who gave their lives to preach the gospel were men of faith, prayer, fasting, and worship.

Throughout this book, we have also referenced men and some women who fasted, prayed, and experienced the supernatural intervention of God in their lives. God has not changed and cannot change. He is still supernaturally moving by the power of the Holy Spirit throughout the world and using men and women to share the gospel message of Christ.

I want to draw your attention to one powerful story in the book entitled *Raised from the Dead* by Evangelist and author Reinhard Bonke.[86] In this book, Reinhard tells the story of a man named Daniel Ekechukwu who had been dead for three days. Daniel's wife felt strongly that God had impressed upon her heart that her husband would be raised to life.

Daniel's wife took her husband to the church via a hearse. The security was tight, and after a struggle with security, she was allowed to take the body of her husband to the church basement, where individuals prayed for him. God performed an incredible miracle that has been more than adequately documented, and Daniel, lying on two wooden tables joined together, began to breathe, even though his body was stiff as iron. As time passed and people began to pray and sing, he eventually stood up and asked for water. This stupendous miracle resulted from his wife's faith, who fasted and believed Hebrews 11:35, "Women received back their dead, raised to life again." Because of this miracle, many have turned to Christ and accepted

DAY 18

him as their Savior. This miracle and Daniel's testimony are continually impacting people throughout the world.

As we fast, pray, worship, and exercise faith in God's Word, we can expect to witness the following:

- **Signs.** The Greek word is *semeia*. Robert Toureville wrote that signs are "pointers toward some significant occurrence. Often, some displayed power which teaches truth are called 'signs.' Signs are used in John's Gospel of the miracles of Jesus."[87] Supernatural intervention, such as signs, attests to God's presence and desire to draw men and women to Him.
- **Wonders.** Here, the Greek word is *terara*. The emphasis is on the effect produced on those viewing the wonder. "Wonders are mouth droppers and eye poppers. Supernatural interventions beyond one's natural understanding inspire men to be in awe of God."[88]
- **Miracles.** A miracle is a supernatural event "which may seem contrary to nature, and which signifies an action in which God reveals himself to man."[89]
- **Gifts of the Holy Spirit.** The New Testament contains different lists of spiritual gifts. In Romans 12:6-8, the Apostle Paul mentions the gifts of prophecy, serving, teaching, encouraging, leadership, and showing mercy. In 1 Corinthians 12:8-10, 27-28, Paul presents the following gifts: The word of wisdom, the word of knowledge, faith, healings, miracles, prophecy, distinguishing between spirits, tongues, interpretation of tongues, apostles, prophets, teachers, helping oth-

ers, and administration. In Ephesians 4:7-11, Paul mentions the gifts of apostles, prophets, evangelists, pastors, and teachers. And in I Peter 4:8-11, the Apostle Peter writes of the gift of hospitality, serving and speaking.

The underlying thought is that whatever spiritual gift of the Spirit a person may exercise, it is for the edification of the body of Christ. I would say that Daniel's wife, Nneka, was graciously given the gift of faith to believe that God would raise her husband from the grave. The tremendous miracle of his resurrection certainly edified and encouraged the body of believers not only in her country but also in countries around the world, in which saints recognize nothing is impossible with God.

DAY 19: FASTING AND THE POURING OUT OF THE SOUL

"...But I have poured out my soul before the Lord."
SAMUEL 1:15, KJV

"True prayer should pour out the whole soul and every inward feeling before him."
-JOHN CALVIN (1509- 1564)

Each year, Elkanah and his two wives went to Shiloh to worship and sacrifice to the Lord. Peninnah had children, but Hannah was barren. When he offered the sacrifice, which was probably a peace offering, he gave the priest his portion, and the remaining portion was given to Peninnah, her sons, and daughters. He gave Hannah a worthy portion because the Lord had shut up her womb and because Peninnah had harassed her for not having children, causing Hannah to be fretful. The sacrifice made to the Lord, and the partaking of the sacrifice, was to be a joyful occasion, but it was not so for Hannah.

As the family sat down to eat, Hannah did not. Her loving husband saw her weeping and not eating and questioned why she was not eating and why her heart was grieved during this time of celebration. Hannah was fasting. "She was in bitterness of soul and prayed unto the Lord and wept sore" (1 Samuel 1:10). She wept and silently prayed before the Lord, her voice muted and only her lips moving as she poured out her soul.

Pouring out your soul before the Lord is what some psychologists would call a cathartic experience. Such an honest and vulnerable act of pouring out your soul before the Lord is a very productive and powerful way to release your pent-up emotions. You'll feel better as you pour out your soul because it reduces stress and brings clarity.

The Holy Spirit has given us insight into her silent prayer. She had made a vow to God that if He would look upon her affliction and remember her by giving her a son, she would dedicate him to the Lord all the days of his life, and no razor would come upon his head. Thus, the dedication would be outwardly visible for all to see!

What captures my heart is her intensity in prayer. She was not just "praying for" an answer to her request; she was, as some dear saints often say, "praying through." What agony of soul, what earnestness, what intensity, what uncompromising sincerity, what determination! She willingly abstained from eating.

Although fasting earns nothing from God, fasting is a complement to prayer. In this scenario, her prayer and fasting vigil was not long. Praying through is more about the quality of our prayer than the quantity of the prayer. She prayed and touched the heart of God.

DAY 19

It does, nevertheless, require "grit." It necessitates moving beyond discouragement and having a laser-like focus on God, who can do "exceedingly abundantly above all we ask or think, according to the power that worketh in us" (Ephesians 3:20, KJV).

Eli, the priest, had observed that her prayer was different and accused her of being drunk. She explained the extremely sorrowful spirit that permitted only the moving of her lips because it was her heart that was fully engaged in the presence of God. The Bible declares, "She spake in her heart only her lips move" (1 Samuel 1:13, KJV). Discovering the whole situation, Eli encouraged her, "Go in peace: and the God of Israel grant thee thy petition that thou hast asked of him" (1 Samuel 1:18, KJV).

The time of prayer and fasting, however long its duration, was over. She asked that she find grace in Eli's sight, and she went her way. Notice the rest of the sentence, and "did eat..." And not only did she eat, but she was happy; and her countenance had changed (See 1 Samuel I:18). The celebration of the sacrifice and the feasting must have still been in place. Her heart is full, and now she can participate in the meal. Shortly after arriving home, she conceived and gave birth to a son. She named him Samuel, meaning "God has heard."

David is another classical illustration of pouring out one's soul. He wrote, "My tears have been my food day and night, while men say to me all day long, 'Where is your God?' These things I remember as I pour out my soul" (Psalm 42:2-3, NIV). The context of this verse is that David is earnestly seeking after God just as the deer seeks for cool, refreshing streams of water. What sincerity, what intensity. He declared his tears were his food day and night (Psalm 42:3, NIV), which indicates that he was fasting and hungering for God.

Aye, and yet, there is a greater than Hannah or David. It is Jesus, the Son of God, who poured out his soul unto death. Isaiah the prophet wrote, "Therefore will I divide him a portion with the great, and he shall divide the spoil with the strong, because he poured out his soul unto death and was numbered among the transgressors" (Isaiah 53:12, ASV). Who can fathom the agony and suffering of Christ on the cross of Calvary for six hours, as he writhed in agony and pain, fasting without food or water, pouring out his soul and crying out, "Father forgive them, for they know not what they do" as his life blood flowed from his hands, his feet, his back, his brow. No greater price was paid for a greater good than the redemption of fallen, sinful humanity.

During these days of prayer and fasting, have you poured your heart out to God? Have you prayed through? Have your tears been your food night and day? If so, believe that the answer is on the way because you know God has heard your prayer and because you know that He is a good and gracious God. Nothing touches the heart of man that does not touch the loving heart of the living Savior.

DAY 20: FASTING AND PRAYING BEFORE GOD

"So it was, when I heard these words, that I sat down and wept, and mourned for many days: I was fasting before the God of Heaven."
NEHEMIAH 1:4, (NKJV)

"But when you fast, put oil on your head and wash your face, so that it will not be obvious to men that you are fasting, but only to your Father, who is unseen; And your Father, who sees what is done in secret, will reward you."
MATTHEW 6:17, NIV

"Prayer is beyond any question the highest activity of the human soul. Man is at his greatest and highest when upon his knees he comes face to face with God."
- DAVID MARTIN LLOYD JONES.

Note the first three words of Nehemiah 1:4: "So it was." In certain circumstances, a crisis or a deep sense of need often precipitates fasting. So it was, in a time when the walls of Jerusalem were broken down, that Nehemiah resorted to praying and fasting for many days. He declared he was praying before the God of heaven.

"So it was," in the time of Queen Esther, during a major crisis, when the extinction of her people (the Jews) was imminent, that she fasted without food and water and prayed before God and found favor before King Ahasuerus and the plot of Haman was revealed, thus rescuing the Jews.

"So it was" when Anna departed not from the temple and served God with fasting and prayer night and day, that a beautiful situation unfolded. Hundreds of years of prophecy was fulfilled as she saw the Christ child and recognized him as the Messiah.

"So it was" when Saul of Tarsus faced a crisis in his life. For three days, fasting, praying, and blinded by a light from heaven brighter than the sun shining around him, he saw a vision of Ananias coming and putting his hand upon him so that he might receive his sight.

"So it was" before Jesus entered public ministry that he was driven by the Holy Spirit into the wilderness to fast and pray before the Father for forty days and forty nights and returned in the power of the Spirit to Galilee.

It is in such times that individuals spend time in the secret presence of God and pour out their hearts before God. Jesus taught that when a person fasts, one should fast and pray before the Father in secret.

When you fast before the face of your Heavenly Father and have been by Him, the face of men need not see you. It is in such times that you can pour out your heart before God. Even though men do not see your tears, God sees them. Even though men do not hear

DAY 20

your voice, God hears it. Hezekiah rejoiced, knowing God saw his tears and heard his voice. Isaiah, the prophet, uttered such comforting words to him that the Lord had heard his prayer and had seen his tears. He was healed from a life-threatening wound or disease.

You, like Nehemiah, have been fasting and praying before God, and Jesus assures you that your Father in Heaven will reward you. Perhaps you may have been fasting and praying to draw closer to God in a more intimate way. Or perhaps like Nehemiah, your heart has been stirred over a desperate situation that only God can change. Take heart, for your Heavenly Father has seen your fasting and heard your prayers. And concerning your weeping, David declared, "You number my wanderings; put my tears in your bottle. Are they not in thy book" (Psalm 56:8, KJV)? David also proclaimed, "I took my troubles to the lord, I cried out to him and he answered my prayer" (Psalm 120:1, ESV).

When you humble your heart before God with prayer and fasting to be seen by the God of heaven and not by men of earth, your heart will be greatly touched by the things that touch the heart of God. How can it not be? God resists the proud, but He gives grace unto the humble.

DAY 21: FASTING AND REVIVAL

"And when they had prayed, the place where they were assembled together was shaken; and they were all filled with the Holly Spirit, and they spoke the word of God with boldness."
ACTS 4:31, KJV

"I believe the power of fasting as it relates to prayer is the spiritual atomic bomb that the Lord has given us to destroy the strongholds of evil and usher in a great revival and spiritual harvest around the world."
-BILL BRIGHT

The Word of God records several revivals that occurred under godly leaders who led the people of Israel to repent of their sins, turn to God, and pray. As we have seen, fasting and prayer are closely linked. A revival under Samuel highlights the elements of repentance, prayer, fasting, and the twelve tribes coming together in unity (1 Samuel 7). Samuel challenged Israel that if they desired to turn to the Lord with all their hearts, they must abandon their idol worship and worship only God. If they made such a resolution, then God would deliver them from the hands of the Philistines.

Samuel gathered the twelve tribes of Israel at Mizpah and informed them he would pray to the Lord for them. There, the people drew water and poured it out before the Lord, symbolizing their repentance and the pouring out of their innermost being, their whole hearts, before Him. They also fasted that day, representing the affliction of their souls, deep and sincere repentance, and the humbling of their hearts before the Lord. Then they confessed that they had sinned against God.

The Philistines observed the uniting of the tribes and their geographical location and "went up against Israel." The Israelites were afraid of the warring Philistines and asked Samuel to pray for them. Samuel called upon the Lord, and the Lord answered him. As Samuel was making a burnt offering with the sacrificial lamb, the Philistines appeared, ready to attack. "But the Lord thundered with a mighty sound that day against the Philistines, threw them into confusion, and they were defeated before Israel" (1 Samuel 7:10, ESV). Samuel commemorated the mighty victory by setting up a stone and naming it "Ebenezer," meaning "stone of help," or "Hitherto hath the Lord helped us" (1 Samuel 7:12, KJV).

God himself has declared in his Word a divine principle, "If my people who are called by My name, humble themselves, and pray and seek My face and turn from their wicked ways, then I will hear from heaven, and for will forgive their sin and heal their land" (II Chronicles 7:14, ESV).

DAY 21

Many revivals have taken place when people unite, humble their hearts, repent, fast, and pray. It is interesting to note how God has used men who were serious about fasting to spark a revival or lead a movement.

Martin Luther (1483-1546)

Martin Luther was a man who believed in fasting and advocated both voluntary and collective fasting. When he was translating the Bible into German, he devoted time to prayer and fasting.[90] It is said that Martin Luther fasted continuously, and his friends feared for his health.[91] Luther launched the Protestant Reformation, insisting that individuals are justified in the sight of God by grace and through the redemptive blood of Jesus Christ. His praying and fasting "brought down God on the dark night of Europe."[92]

Jonathan Edwards (1703-1758)

Edwards maintained daily set times for prayer that he set aside for solitude, meditation, and fasting. But prayer was not just a compartment in his daily routine, an exercise that possessed little connection with the rest of his hours alone. Rather, he sought to make his study itself a sanctuary, and whether wrestling with Scripture, preparing sermons, or writing in his notebooks, he worked as a worshipper. "Thought, prayer, and writing were all woven together" (*Jonathan Edwards: A New Biography*, 143).[93]

John Wesley (1703-1758)

John Wesley was the 15th of 19 children born to Samuel and Susan Wesley. Of her 19 children, only nine lived beyond infancy. He attended Lincoln College and was ordained an Anglican priest in 1728. Charles, John, along with other students, formed a group called the "Holy Club." John and Charles fasted every Wednesday and Friday until 3:00 p.m. Due to the various requirements and methods of the group, an anonymous author of a pamphlet gave them the name Methodist.

Richard Foster, quoting John Wesley on the subject, wrote, "It was not merely by the light of reason...that the people of God have been, in all ages, directed to used fasting as a means, ... but they have been... taught it of God himself, by clear and open revelations of his will..."[94]

The unregenerate, such as Buddhists and Muslims, fast as well as regenerate men. Although John Wesley had chosen the path of being a minister, was ordained, practiced such disciplines as reading the Bible, praying, and fasting, he was not born again of the Spirit. It was in April 1735, as Reverend Samuel Wesley (John's father) was dying, that he turned his face toward John and spoke, "The inward witness, son, the inward witness, is the strongest proof of Christianity."[95]

Around October 1736, Bishop August Spangenberg challenged John with a question while walking along a beach in Georgia, "Does the Spirit of God bear witness with your spirit that you are a child of God?"[96] John could only reply that he knew Jesus was the Savior of the world. The Moravian Bishop agreed Jesus is the Savior of the

DAY 21

world, but further asked, "But do you know He has saved you?"[97]

These were seed thoughts that would later lead to Wesley's conversion. John would travel to Georgia to do missionary work. He wrote before leaving, "...I who went to America to convert others, was never myself converted."[98] However, on the 24th, of May 1738, the message of salvation by grace through faith was embraced. Wesley noted in his journal that as he heard someone reading Luther's preface to the book of Romans, he understood how God works in a man's heart through faith, stating: "I felt, I did trust in Christ, Christ alone for salvation; and the assurance was given to me that he had taken away *my* sins, even *mine*, and saved me from the law of sin and death."[99]

Fasting and prayer would no longer be a meritorious act in his life. It was New Year. In 1738-1739, John Wesley met with a group of seven Methodist men and sixty other fervent Christians who had planned an all-night prayer service and would dine on only bread and water. Describing the event, Wesley wrote:

> About three in the morning, as we were continuing instant in prayer, the power of God came mightily upon us, insomuch that many cried out for exceeding joy, and many fell to the ground. As soon as we were recovered a little from the awe and amazement at the presence of His majesty we broke out with one voice, 'We praise Thee, O God, we acknowledge Thee to be the Lord![100]

In 1743 John Wesley wrote a document entitled *The Nature, Design and General Rules of the United Societies*. In lieu of our subject matter on fasting and prayer, it is interesting to observe the last paragraph of the document expressed the expectation that individuals would attend public worship, minister the word of God that was read or expounded, along with searching the Scriptures, observing communion, having family and private *prayer,* and practicing fasting and abstinence.[101]

In their book, *John Wesley*, Janet and Geoff Benge stated that Wesley, during his lifetime, rode 250,000 miles on horseback and preached over forty thousand sermons. His *Collective Works,* which he published, filled thirty-two volumes.[102] In addition, Wesley produced four hundred books, learned ten languages, and, at eighty-three, became annoyed when he could not write for more than fifteen hours a day without hurting his eyes. At eighty-six, he felt ashamed that he could not preach more than twice a day. He complained in his diary about an increasing tendency to lie in bed until 5:30 in the morning.[103] What a remarkable life and ministry that fasting and prayer must have contributed!

Charles Finney (1792-1875)

Charles Finney (1792-1875), the great revivalist who played a significant role in the Second Great Awakening, found it was personally profitable "to hold frequent days of private fasting" for "kindling "a revival in our soul" as a remedy to a flagging spirit of prayer and for gaining "greater prevalence with God.[104] Finney tells how, when a revival began to decline in power, they would set aside time for fasting and prayer, and inevitably, the work of God would surge

DAY 21

ahead once more.[105]

In her book entitled *Fasting for Fire, Jennifer A. Miskov* wrote that Charles Finney, "Prepared for revivals by organizing teams to pray fast and spread the word before he arrived."[106] Finney had a great prayer warrior by the name of Daniel Nash, who would precede Finney's arrival weeks or months ahead of the meeting and would pray and fast for the meetings.

The preaching career of Charles Finney would see approximately 500,000 people come to Christ. Notable was the revival in 1831, in which 100,000 people were converted in Rochester New York.[107]

Billy Graham (1918- 2018)

Billy Graham preached to an estimated 215 million people at live events and crusades, with an estimated 2.2 million people responding to invitations to become Christians.[108] On fasting, he wrote, "In the same way that time with God and time in the Word is crucial to our spiritual development, this discipline is key to our growth."[109] One can only imagine how much fasting and prayer contributed to such a powerful ministry and the entrance of souls into the kingdom of God.

Rinehard Bonnke (1940- 2019)

You may or may not have heard of Reinhard Bonnke. He was a great German-American Pentecostal evangelist who believed in prayer and fasting. At the age of nine, he found Christ as his Savior and heard the call of God before he was a teenager to be a missionary to Africa. In 1967, he began his missionary activity to Africa. The largest recorded attendance in such an open-air meeting was in the city of Lagos, Africa, during the "Millennium Crusade in November 2000, when over 1.6 million people thronged the field to hear the Gospel!"[110] He left a great spiritual legacy. According to Christ for all Nations, there is "documented 97,076,859 decisions for Christ and counting."[111]

Saints Today

We reiterate we cannot merit any action of God through fasting. In fasting, we humble ourselves before God, give Him our attention, attempt to align our will with His, our heart with Him, and share with Him our desperate situation and challenges. We have an excellent opportunity to be used by God and accomplish his sovereign will. Fasting and praying, humbling our hearts before God, open our hearts to the available opportunities. It allows us to be vessels in the hands of the Master Potter and to be used for His glory.

I would like to mention some of the great revivals that were birthed through prayer and fasting. Before doing so, I would like to reference William T. Stead, who quoted Dr. F. B. Meyer, who stated, "The supreme test of a revival is the ethical result.[112] The fruit of revival will bring a change in the moral fabric of an individual and the community. William T. Stead wrote, concerning revival:

> And when it comes to be looked at scientifically, who can deny that a great religious Revival often succeeds in achieving the result which we all desire more rapidly, more decisively, and in a

DAY 21

greater number of cases, than any other agency known to mankind? We may discount it as much as we like. But the facts are there. It is not necessary to credit the Revival with all the results which it reveals, any more than we may credit a day's sunshine in spring with all the flowers it brings forth. But it brings them out. So does a Revival. [113]

The Welsh Revival (1904-1905)

The Welsh Revival was a powerful spiritual awakening. People often link it to a period of intense prayer and fasting. One of the key figures was Evan Roberts. It is also said that "Evan Roberts and his young group of saints prayed and fasted for five years. God moved his hand over Wales, and the great Welsh revival took place."[114] G. Campbell Morgan wrote that in 1904 on Christmas Day, "Practically the whole of Wales was on its knees, probably every chapel in the principality was open, and was filled. In some towns which I visited there were monster demonstrations. Certain churches had combined for united processions, and in some cases the paraders marched the whole night long.[115]

According to newspaper reports of the day, the Welsh Revival spread from Europe first, then America and eventually to all five continents. Some missionaries from Wales traveled to Madagascar, India, China and Patagonia and promoted and confirmed the Revival. Colleges provided the personnel for overseas missions and helped create a spirit of prayer for an awakening. The Welsh Revival produced a worldwide movement in the church.[116] Although the revival lasted less than a year, 100,000 souls were converted. The movement spread to Scotland and England, and it is estimated that a million people were converted.[117]

Concerning the man, Evan Roberts, Dr. G. Campbell Morgan wrote, "God has set his hand upon the lad, beautiful in simplicity, ordained in his devotion, lacking all the qualities that we have looked for in preachers and prophets and leaders."

The Apostle Paul wrote, "But God hath chosen the foolish things of the world to confound the wise, and God hath chosen the weak things of the world to confound the things which are mighty. And the base things of the world and the things which are despised, hath God chosen, yea and the things which are not, to bring to naught the things that are that no flesh should glory in his presence" (1 Corinthians 1:27-29, KJV).

The Pyongyang Revival 1907

It is interesting to note that Korean Christians heard of the Welsh Revival, had a great desire for the same blessings of God, and in 1907, the Pyongyang Revival, or the Great Pyongyang Revival, took place. God used R.A. Hartie a Canadian physician and a Methodist missionary, and Kil Sonchu, a Presbyterian minister, during this movement.[118]

The Azusa Revival (April 9, 1906-1915)

The Azusa Street Revival was a historic revival that began on April 09, 1906. It began in Los Angeles, California, and was led by Rev.

DAY 21

William J. Seymour, who was an African American preacher. The revival continued scribers until about 1915.[119] "Word of the revival was spread abroad through *The Apostolic Faith*, a paper that Seymour sent to some 50,000 subscribers. So many missionaries spread the word from Azusa that within two years the movement had spread to fifty countries."[120] Azusa Street Revival was the birthplace of the Pentecostal Movement. It is estimated that there are 600 million Pentecostal and Charismatic believers. Scholars estimate that by the year 2025, 30% of Christians will be Pentecostal-Charismatic[121]

A book by Franklin Hall, published in 1947 and later published in 2016 by Matio Fine Books in 2016, revealed some interesting thoughts concerning the importance of fasting, prayer, associated with the Azusa Street Revival, He wrote, "A few people came to Los Angeles in 1906 and started a ten-day fasting and prayer season, and the Holy Spirit fell."[122] Hall wrote about the time he preached at the Azusa Temple, which was the original church of the Azusa people moved to. He stated he spoke to Mother Cotton, who commented that she had fasted when the power fell forty years earlier and that "Many of the major miracles, baptisms, and manifestations of the power of God were traced directly to the much FASTING and PRAYER."[123] She also stated, "The first thing that was done before the power fell on Azusa was a united ten-day season of fasting and prayer. If there was any sectarianism, fasting broke it down."[124]

Franklin had the opportunity to talk to another of the old-time Azusa pillars of faith, Glen Cook. Cook commented he had a room adjoining Brother Seymore, a leader of the Azusa folk, who fasted for weeks at a time. He informed Franklin that there was much fasting and prayer in those days. Another Azusa Street worker, Brother Thomas, stated, "It had to be prayer and fasting before God came down in this wise. He heard their earnest, fervent cry, and then He came on the scene."[125]

Yet another participant in the Azusa revival was A.W. Dodson, who told Franklin, "They just waited on the Lord in fastings, prayer, and the unity of the Spirit. He further stated, "The Holy Spirit was there in operation, and this was brought about through intense closeness and communion with God by everyone forgetting about food and their cares. We just drank at the Fountain of the Spirit."[126]

Tacoma, Washington Revival (1946-1947)

Franklin Hall writes of the revival that took place in Tacoma, Washington, in which the whole city was shaken. Thousands of people were saved, healed, and baptized. Hall attributed the revival to an extensive amount of fasting and prayer. Members of his evangelistic team fasted ten days, sixteen days, and most fasted twenty-one days.[127] Hall stated that he had spoken to fifty thousand people about fasting and prayer, and one million pieces of literature were distributed on the subject of fasting.[128]

The Brownsville Revival

The revival began on Father's Day, June 18, 1995, at an Assembly of God church in Pensacola, Florida. More than four million people attended the revival meetings from 1995 to 2000. Two years before

DAY 21

the revival, in 1993, Pastor John Kilpatrick encouraged his church to pray for revival.[129]

During the revival, fasting and prayer were contributing elements. Fasting and prayer were a means of prioritizing God over physical desires, deepening their relationship with God, aligning their personal and corporate desires in accord with God's will, and expressing an intense spiritual hunger for his presence and intervention. During the revival, nearly 200,000 people accepted Christianity, and by the fall of 2000, over 1,000 people who experienced the revival were enrolled at the Brownsville Revival School of Ministry.[130]

CLOSING THOUGHT

Throughout history, we have observed that God hears the heart's cry of his people as they fast and pray with the right motivation. If you have just completed a 21-day journey of prayer and fasting, your heart may have experienced a yearning for more of God and a willingness to be a vessel used by God. You may have also been praying and fasting to see God sovereignly, graciously, and powerfully move in your life, your church, your community, and throughout the world.

As your journey of 21 days of prayer and fasting comes to an end, you are cognizant that there is nothing miraculous about the number 21. However, you are fully cognizant that there is an omnipotent God who has heard your prayers, who has seen your tears.

A seed, in the natural aspect, is sown in hope of a harvest. It lies in the earth's darkness as the soil, sunshine, and rain contribute in time to its germination, growth, and fruitfulness. So, in the realm of spirit, you have sown spiritual seeds of prayer and fasting. In time, our sovereign God will water the seed. In time, it will grow, and in time it will not fail to bring forth fruit in the kingdom of God. I want to encourage you not to be discouraged or doubt the effectiveness of these 21 days of prayer and fasting. Instead, courageously and confidently embrace the Word of God, which declares, "But without faith it is impossible to please him, for he that cometh to God must believe that he is, and that he is a REWARDER of them that diligently seek him" (Hebrews 11:6, KJV).

ENDNOTES

1 Jennifer A. Miskov, Fasting for Fire (Shippensburg: Destiny Image Publishers INC., 2021),99.

2 Baker Encyclopedia of Psychology & Counseling. David G. Benner & Peter C. Hill, editors (Grand Rapids: Baker Books, 1999), 450.

3 Mary Ruth Swope, The Roots & Fruits of Fasting (New Kensington: Whitaker House, 1998).

4 https://www.cslewisinstitute.org/resources/the-place-of-fasting-in-the-christian-life/#:~:text=Fasting%20shows%20God%20that%20we,He%20may%20or%20may%20not.

5 Jentezen Franklin, Fasting: Opening the door to a deeper, more intimate, more powerful relationship with God (Lake Mary: Charisma House, 2023) 113.

6 https://news.americafirst.com/the-power-of-pulling-together/

7 Jennifer A. Miskov, Fasting for Fire (Shippensburg: Destiny Image Publishers, INC., 2021), 99-100.

8 Baker Encyclopedia of the Bible, Walter A. Elwell, Ed. (Volume 1, p. 233, Grand Rapids, 1988, p.233).

9 Richard Foster, Celebration of Discipline: The Path to Spiritual Growth (London: Hodder, 1989) 62-63.

10 Charles Spurgeon, Spurgeon on Prayer & Spiritual Warfare (New Kensington: Whitaker House, 1998), 270.

11 Dick Eastman, The Change the World School of Prayer (Colorado Springs: Every Home for Christ, 2017), 165).

12 Arthur Wallis, God's Chosen Fast: A Spiritual and Practical Guide to Fasting (Fort Washington, CLC Publications: 2024), 27.

13 Jentezen Franklin, Fasting: Opening the door to a deeper, more intimate, more powerful relationship with God (Lake Mary, Charisma House: 2023) p. 32.

14 https://www.medicalnewstoday.com/articles/325174#effects

15 Jentezen Franklin, Fasting: Opening the door to a deeper more intimate, more powerful relationship with God (Lake Mary: Charisma, 2023), 42.

16 Arthur Wallis, God's Chosen Fast.

17 Walter H. Beuttler, Answers to Questions on Fasting and Prayer: Bulletin insert (1971).

18 Andrew Murray (Revised by Harold J Chadwick) With Christ in the School of Prayer, Gainesville: Bridge-Logos Publishers,1999),102.

19 Jentezen Franklin, Fasting: Opening the door to a deeper, more intimate, more powerful relationship with God (Carisma House: Lake Mary, 2023), 112.

20 Robert Tourville, The Acts of the Apostles: A Verse-By-Verse Commentary from The Classical Pentecostal Point of View (New Wilmington, House of Bon Giovanni: 1983), 176.

21 Ibid, p. 176

22 James Strong, The Strongest Strong's Exhaustive Concordance of the Bible, (Grand Rapids, Zondervan 2001).

23 https://www.foodingodsplace.com/fasting-calling-naaman-complex/

24 https://www.cslewisinstitute.org/resources/the-place-of-fasting-in-the-christian-life/#:~:text=Fasting%20shows%20God%20that%20we,He%20may%20or%20may%20not.

25 https://ccel.org/ccel/murray/prayer/prayer.XIII.html

26 https://www.youtube.com/hashtag/fastingandfaith

27 Arthur Wallis, God's Chosen Fast: A Spiritual and Practical Guide to Fasting (Fort Washington, CLC Publications, 2024), 49.

28 A. W. Tozer, The Essential Tozer Collection: Compiled by James L. Snyder, (Minneapolis, Bethany House: 2013), 15.

29 Elmer L. Towns, Fasting for Spiritual Breakthrough: A Practical Guide to Nine Biblical Fasts (Bethany House: Minneapolis, 2017), 243

30 Charles A. Rhodus, Fasting Secrets Revealed: Breakthrough Fasting (Orlando, Charles H. Rhodus: 2020), 23.

31 https://cepadnica.org/the-lesson-of-the-mustard-seed/#:~:text=Matthew%2013%3A31%2D21%20",and%20perch%20in%20its%20branches."

32 https://www.biblestudytools.com/bible-study/topical-studies/what-it-looks-like-to-have-the-faith-of-a-mustard-seed.html#:~:text=Their%20seeds%20are%20very%20small,that%20He%20has%20for%20them.

33 Ibid., 22.

34 Ibid., 26

35 A. Lukyn Williams, Pulpit Commentary: Matthew, (Grand Rapids: Wm. B. Eerdmans Publishing Company, 1961), 178.

36 Richard Foster, Celebration of Discipline: The Path to Spiritual Growth (London, Hodder: 2008), 68.

37 Ibid., 68.

38 Ibid., 68.

39 James Strong, The Strongest Strong's Exhaustive Concordance: Exhaustive Concordance of the Bible (Grand Rapids: Zondervan, 2001).

40 Andrew Murray (Revised by Harold J. Chadwick), With Christ in

the School of Prayer (Gainesville: Bridge-Logos Publishers,1999), 101-102,

41 Robert Tourville, Acts of the Apostles: A Verse by Verse Commentary from The Classical Pentecostal Point of View (New Washington: House of BonGiovanni, 1983), 235-236).

42 J. Hudson Taylor, Jay Hudson Taylor An Autobiography (Florida: ReadaClassic.com. 2010).

43 Mark Batterson, The Circle Maker: Praying Circles Around Your Biggest Dreams and Greatest Fears (Grand Rapids: Zondervan, 2016.

44 Ibid, p. 33-34.

45 Richard Foster, Celebration of Discipline (London: Hodder), 67.

46 Ibid.

47 https://en.wikipedia.org/wiki/Ancient_Egyptian_cuisine

48 https://en.wikipedia.org/wiki/Ancient_Egyptian_cuisine

49 https://biblehub.com/commentaries/1_samuel/2-29.htm

50 John Piper, A Hunger for God: Desiring God through Fasting and Prayer (Wheaton: Crossway, 2013), 11.

51 https://www.kneillfoster.com/art19/Fasting.php

52 https://ezraproject.com/ekkakeo-too-soon-to-quit/

53 A.W. Tozer, The Fire of God's Presence, compiled and edited by James L. Snyder (Bethany House: Minneapolis, 2020), 177.

54 Jim Cymbala, Breakthrough Prayer (Grand Rapids: Zondervan.)

55 Richard Foster, Celebration of Discipline (London: Hodder & Stoughton Ltd, 2008), 73.

56 Mark Batterson, The Circle Maker: Praying Circles Around Your Biggest Dreams and Greatest Fears (Grand Rapids: Zondervan, 2016), 174.

57 Andrew Murray, (Revised by Harold J. Chadwick) With Christ in

the School of Prayer (Gainesville: Bridge Logos Publishers, 1999), 102.

58 Elmer Towns, Fasting for Spiritual Breakthrough: A Practical Guide to Nine Biblical Fasts (Minneapolis: Bethany House, 2017), 15.

59 Jim Cymbala, Breakthrough Prayer: The Power of Connecting with the Heart of God (Grand Rapids: Zondervan, 2003), 129-130.

60 Mary Ruth Swope, The Roots & Fruits of Fasting (New Kensington: Whitaker, 2013), 64.

61 Ibid., 65

62 Don Colbert, MD, Fasting Zone: Reset Your Health and Cleanse Your Body in 21 Days (Lake Mary: Siloam, 2020), 4.

63 https://www.healthline.com/nutrition/fasting-benefits#:~:text=Generally%2C%20most%20fasts%20are%20performed,loss%20and%20better%20brain%20function.

64 Elmer L Towns, Fasting for Spiritual Breakthrough: Nine Biblical Fast (Minneapolis: Bethany House, 2017), 211.

65 https://www.singlecare.com/blog/news/stress-statistics/

66 https://www.psychiatry.org/news-room/news-releases/annual-poll-adults-express-increasing-anxiousness

67 Arthur Wallis, God's Chosen Fast: A Spiritual and Practical Guide to Fasting (Fort Washington: MaCLC Publications, 2024), 111.

68 Jentezen Franklin, Fasting: Opening the door to a deeper more intimate, more powerful relationship with God (Lake Mary: Charisma House, 2023), 42.

69 Mary Ruth Swope, The Roots & Fruits of Fasting (South Avinger: Swoop Engerprises, LLC, 1998), 54.

70 Ibid, 54.

71 Martin Llyod Jones, Romans Chapters 3:20 -4:25 (Grand Rapids: Zondervan Publishing House, 1976), 82.

72 Ibid.

73 Luke 11:5-7, NIV.

74 Dick Eastman, The Change the Word School of Prayer (Colorada Springs: Every Home for Christ), 193). Author of the quote unknown.

75 David G. Benner & Peter C. Hill, (Baker Encyclopedia of Psychology & Counseling, 2nd ed., Grand Rapids: Baker Books, 1999), 326.

76 A.T. Robertson, Word Pictures in the New Testament, Vol. 5 (Nashville: Broadman Press, 1931), 203.

77 https://www.goodreads.com >work>115916-spurgeon.

78 A.T. Robertson, Word Pictures in the New Testament. Vol. 5 (Nashville: Broadman Press, 1931), 23-24.

79 J. B. Phillips, The New Testament in Modern English (MacMillian: New York, 1958).

80 Jentezen Franklin, Fasting (Lake Mary: Charisma House, 2023), 106.

81 Walter H. Beuttler, Waiting on the Lord (Deeper Life Press, 2023).

82 Ibid.

83 Dave Patterson, Pursuit: 21-Day Prayer & Fasting Devotional Orlando: (The Father's House.org, 2025), 76.

84 Andrew Murray, Waiting on God (New York: Cosimo, Inc: 2007), 13.

85 https://www.azquotes.com/quotes/topics/holy-spirit.html

86 Rinehard Bonke, Dead from the Dead: The Miracle That Brigs Promise to America (Longwood: Whitaker House, 2014).

87 Robert A. Tourville, The Acts of the Apostles (New Wilmington: House of Bon Giovanni, 1983), 40.

88 Ibid, p. 40.

89 Walter A. Elwell Baker Encyclopedia of the Bible, Vol. 3 (Grand Rapids: Baker Books, 1988), 1468.

90 Mahesh Chavda, The Hidden Power of Prayer & Fasting, Shippensburg: Destiny Image, 1998), 144-145.

91 https://www.gods-acres.com/uploads/5/1/3/0/51300023/fasting.handout.pdf

92 https://www.gods-acres.com/uploads/5/1/3/0/51300023/fasting.handout.pdf

93 https://biblicalspiritualitypress.org/2018/05/15/doing-your-work-prayerfully-a-lesson-from-jonathan-edwards/#:~:text="Edwards%20maintained%20daily%20set%20timesthe%20cost%20of%20his%20health.

94 Richard Foster, Celebration of Discipline (London: Holder & Stoughton Ltd, 2008), 73.

95 Janet and Geoff Benge, Jonathan Wesley: The World His Parish (Seattle: YWAM Publishers, 2007), 65.

96 Ibid., 80.

97 Ibid., 81.

98 Ibid., 90.

99 Ibid., 100.

100 Ibid., 106.

101 Janet and Geoff Benge, John Wesley: The World His Parish (Seattle: YWAM,2007), 138.

102 Ibid., 168.

103 https://ministry127.com/resources/illustration/john-wesley

104 https://asburyseminary.edu/news/fasting-prayer-awakeni https://en.wikipedia.org/wiki/Encyclopediang/

105 https://asburyseminary.edu/news/fasting-prayer-awakening/

106 Jennifer A. Miskov, Fasting for Fire (Shippensburg: Destiny Image Publishers, 2021), 17.

107 https://pastorvlad.org/awakening/

108 https://research.lifeway.com/2018/02/21/billy-grahams-life-minis-

try-by-the-numbers/#:~:text=215%20million%20–%20estimated%20number%20of,invitations%20to%20become%20a%20Christian.

109 https://billygraham.org/articles/waste-time-wisely-fasting

110 https://cfan.org/reinhard-bonnke

111 Ibid.

112 William T. Stead & G. Campbell Morgan, The Welsh Revival & The Story of the Welsh Revival, (Lawton: Trumpet Press, 2017), 62.

113 Ibid, p. 63.

114 https://www.gods-acres.com/uploads/5/1/3/0/51300023/fasting.handout.pdf

115 William T. Stead & G./ Campbell Morgan, The Welsh Revival & The Story of the Welsh Revival by Eye Witnesses (Lawton: Trumpet Press, 2017), 141.

116 https://atwistedcrownofthorns.com/2018/01/22/the-effects-of-the-1904-welsh-revival/#:~:text=The%20Revival%20importantly%20produced%20a,Related%20articles:

117 Ibid.

118 https://en.wikipedia.org/wiki/Pyongyang_Revival

119 https://en.wikipedia.org/wiki/Azusa_Street_Revival

120 https://www.pbs.org/thisfarbyfaith/journey_3/p_9.html

121 https://www.andrewkgabriel.com/2017/09/26/how-many-pentecostals/#:~:text=How%20Many%20Pentecostals%20are%20There,includes%2011.8%20million%20Oneness%20Christians.

122 Franklin Hall, The Fasting Prayer (Eastford: Martina Fine Books, 2016), 26.

123 Ibid, p. 27.

124 Ibid.

125 Ibid.

126 Ibid.

127 Ibid.

128 Ibid.

129 https://en.wikipedia.org/wiki/Brownsville_Revival

130 https://en.wikipedia.org/wiki/Brownsville_Revival

www.ingramcontent.com/pod-product-compliance
Lightning Source LLC
Chambersburg PA
CBHW060529080526
44586CB00012B/670